Floral arrangements based on

# Principles

# of Floral Design

Gregor Lersch

FDF

FLORALDESIGN EDITION

# Contents

| | |
|---|---|
| Fundamental principles for floral arrangements | 4 |
| Arrangement categories | 5 |
| Order guideline for arrangement categories | 7 |
| **Category** | 8 |
| Symmetrical | 9 |
| Asymmetrical | 9 |
| **Arrangement** | 10 |
| Decorative | 11 |
| Vegetative | 12 |
| Formal-linear | 13 |
| **Line arrangement** | 14 |
| Radial line arrangement | 16 |
| Parallel line arrangement | 17 |
| Diagonal line arrangement | 18 |
| Winding line arrangement | 19 |
| Crossing line arrangement | 20 |
| Free line arrangement | 21 |
| **Position of the center of growth/focal point** | 22 |
| Center of growth below the container | 23 |
| Center of growth in the container | 23 |
| Center of growth above the container | 24 |
| Center of growth beside the container | 24 |
| **Number and arrangement of growth centers/** | |
| **focal point** | 25 |
| One center of growth/focal point | 26 |
| Several centers of growth/focal points | 26 |
| Several centers of growth/focal points in | |
| liberal arrangement | 27 |
| **Proportions** | 28 |
| Proportions directed upward | 29 |
| Proportions directed downward | 29 |
| Proportions directed horizontally | 30 |
| Proportions directed diagonally | 30 |
| Proportions directed symmetrically | 31 |

| | |
|---|---|
| **Structural Designing** | 32 |
| Structured | 33 |
| Textured | 34 |
| Designed | 35 |
| Object-like | 36 |
| Layered | 37 |
| Stacked | 38 |
| Winding | 39 |
| Interwoven | 40 |
| Bundled | 41 |
| Grading | 42 |
| | |
| **Arrangements** | 46 |
| | |
| Thanks | 220 |
| Imprint | 218 |

## Fundamental Principles for Floral Arrangements

This book attempts to develop an appropriate method for the professional arrangement of flowers based on guidelines which have become recognized worldwide. Expert knowledge is systematically organized. What has been already learned and taught is thoughtfully examined, providing a clear guideline by which to delve into expert knowledge about floristry and flower design. Clearly defined terms ensure a mutual language and thus facilitate communication – worldwide. Nonetheless, rules and regulations are avoided as much as possible so that in developing a personal floral design, the designer has as much leeway as possible, subject only to the principles prescribed by nature. Nature is the master, teaching us how and what to do. Floral arrangements are based on the knowledge of plants, their environment and their characteristics ranging from growth to drying, irrespective of whether such arrangements copy, abstract from or consciously ignore nature.

**Floral design requires a terminology.**

## Arrangement Categories

The present guidelines of design categories deal, first of all, with two basic elements of an arrangement: symmetry and asymmetry, which again and again demand the very first major decision from the floral designer. Variations in design depend upon whether the designer presents the plants or the floral arrangements according to the laws of nature, or whether a new shape is designed by a floral architect. The third dimension of the arrangement deals with the clear depiction of the plants, the shape of the flower, its lines and contours. The guidelines presented here show possible general line structures in floral oeuvres. To provide assistance to the student, the regularity of the line structure is defined. The horizontal and vertical position of the center of growth must be distinctly visible in the arrangement. The so-called proportions describe the physical extension of the arrangement as seen from the anchor or base of growth. Where is the center of growth? Where the vanishing point? And how many of these can an arrangement have? The description of the structures serves the purpose of ensuring that the creative variety is not seen as a chaotic flood of imagery but helps to explain it in a logical manner. The guidelines are to link the different design criteria with one another and show what is compatible and what is not. Floral arrangements thus described can be better comprehended. The profession of a florist is given a distinct and generally reliable language without restricting or suppressing creative individuality.

Any new terms which prove sensible should naturally be added to this guideline. This is the reason why the principles of the floral arrangement must be revised every now and then as to their completeness, and if necessary supplemented. This is the only way to achieve a continuity of further development in the profession. The arrangement models shown in this book can only be seen as excerpts from a plethora of variations presented in the guideline. Naturally, they are subjective interpretations.

**To design implies to arrange – and whenever a floral material is already provided by nature, it is for the floral designer to do just that: to arrange.**

"Dull", hypothetical floral examples are hardly possible. Personal preferences and views will again and again creep in, such as the delight in the movement of plants or branches or fibers which simultaneously soften and change an arrangement, by blurring its distinct criteria and breaking its hard edges. The various interpretations may easily extend to the boundaries of the next category. That is, a decorative work can easily explore the realm both of the formal and of the vegetative. However, as long as a single "category" prevails and dominates the design, the arrangement has recognition value. And this is what it is all about: Being able to recognize the design criteria applied. It should be possible to reveal and to teach the significant elements of an arrangement.

Perhaps creativity can be given new impulses by means of a clear presentation of the art of floral arrangement by indicating the options available for various combinations so as to counteract mere duplication. The aim is, by making a calculated decision, to create order and design by consciously referring to lines for new impulses for the positioning of the center of growth, the proportions and the structures by benefiting from the entire spectrum, and developing one's very own personal, eternally young style due to floral versatility.

The heart and soul of the arrangement which emphasizes the beauty of the flowers can be created only through the personal artistic charisma and seductiveness of the floral arranger. To promote these elements, other factors are required, such as stylistics, theory of color, art and design studies, architectural knowledge, fashion influences, etc. Dealing with these different fields of knowledge and elements of style leads to a required general aesthetic education and the realization that any work of art has a history and can never be without a 'face'.

Sound knowledge of a cultural context extends the range of one's own design options, just like measures for developing personality and creativity. The aim of this book is to move floral design out of the realm of the pure feeling and genius of a select few and into a more accessible arena, that of clearly-stated, comprehensible principles of design which at the same time promote creativity, facilitate the learning process and increase global communication.

**This book concentrates fully on the graphic principles of design as they can contribute to an understanding of the art of floristry, over and above a mere emotional or faddish effect.**

# Guideline of Arrangement Categories

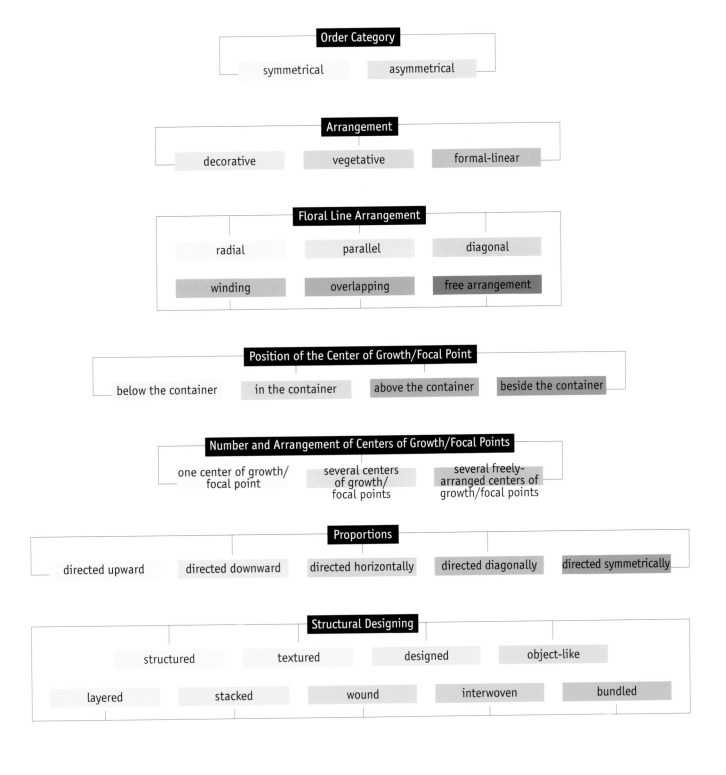

**Order Category**
- symmetrical
- asymmetrical

**Arrangement**
- decorative
- vegetative
- formal-linear

**Floral Line Arrangement**
- radial
- parallel
- diagonal
- winding
- overlapping
- free arrangement

**Position of the Center of Growth/Focal Point**
- below the container
- in the container
- above the container
- beside the container

**Number and Arrangement of Centers of Growth/Focal Points**
- one center of growth/ focal point
- several centers of growth/ focal points
- several freely-arranged centers of growth/focal points

**Proportions**
- directed upward
- directed downward
- directed horizontally
- directed diagonally
- directed symmetrically

**Structural Designing**
- structured
- textured
- designed
- object-like
- layered
- stacked
- wound
- interwoven
- bundled

## Order Category

The first and most important decision to be made by the floral designer when choosing materials concerns the order category. Careful consideration of the environment of the arrangement is required here: style, architecture, Zeitgeist, and the historical style of a room all influence the decision regarding the order category. Is the arrangement intended for an official occasion, or for a more private and intimate event? Is it to be emotionally light or solemn? Exuberant, highly representative or simply an impromptu decoration? The well-considered choice of the order category already equals a statement – it permits the portrayal of different types of people, and enables the arrangement to reflect occasions and seasons. The scope of possible effects ranges from military or even heraldic rigidity to unconventional liberal spontaneity.

Selecting flowers, containers and possible decorative items and accessories requires a sure instinct on the part of the floral designer on what is appropriate and suitable for whatever occasion. It is very often observed that florists are fascinated by the very effect and charisma of florals and that, due to inadequate knowledge and mastery of the order categories or simply due to a lack of concentration, they abandon the entire design-related consistency. Moreover, there is a certain grading in the order categories. For example, an inflexible symmetry may appear unattractive, empty and unnatural in a floral sense. Here, the conscious attempt of combining both order categories may help. Yet it is important that one of the two components is clearly the dominating design and leads the way. Such clear domination particularly counts when various definitions of the arrangement guideline are going to be combined.

## Symmetrical

Symmetry stands for a mirrored reproduction, two congruent halves separated by a central axis. Symmetry refers not only to volume, dimension, and visual weighting, but also to shapes and colors that are diffused evenly throughout two halves of a room, a scene or a picture. Symmetry is also defined as "strict order", with its roots vested in the old high cultures of this world. From Classical to Medieval times, throughout the Neoclassical Age and even until long into our century, the principle of symmetry appears to dominate and determine whatever is official and representative. The art of religions, the mighty and the powerful, the environment of power and all occasions where people gathered for a festive and collective deed found their characteristic expression in symmetry.

In floristry, symmetry often faces pragmatic obstacles such as natural growth variations or irregularities of the material. The majority of florals are not symmetrical – as if challenging the creative liberty of spontaneous asymmetry. The skills of the floral arranger are called for here, to compensate the inner structure of an arrangement either by correcting the exterior contour or by displacing the emphasis. The symmetrical order category has the advantage that this allows for easier interpretation of a man-made, direct and nearly mathematical balance. Some find dealing with symmetry easier than others; it is very often a metaphor for "order" – or even, as the recorded term states, "the strict order." More often than not, however, this order category is a great challenge to the kind of manual dexterity that is required when creating an even contour and a clean symmetry. That is because symmetry does not facilitate the handling of and experienced play with the disciplines. The effect of symmetry is not very elaborate since symmetrical arrangements appear more controllable and self-controlled than their counterpart, i.e. liberal arrangements. The static challenge of a symmetrical arrangement is less demanding – it tends to rest in itself.

## Asymmetrical

There is no visual center, no opportunity for a mirrored reproduction here. There is no evenness in asymmetry; no expanse, no structure, no placement in the outline, not a trace of regularity – nothing is identical, nothing appears more than once. Asymmetrical arranging requires discipline since any liberal arrangement also calls for some structure in order to be meaningful. The order of asymmetry is a three-dimensional order, with harmonious proportions created within that order. For example, a simple combination of "much" and "little" floral material to design an asymmetrical arrangement is not enough. Only the correct mathematical formula – such as a 3:5:8 ratio – can evoke the effect of harmony. A further difficulty is that such relations should not be designed as a relief, but instead in a confident sculptural manner extending into the room. Asymmetrical space and thus asymmetrical arrangements only have a single dominant trait. Symmetry, however, may feature various balanced guidelines.

Asymmetry was the preferred order category of Modernism and is apparent in many creative forms of design.

In architecture, e.g., it hardly requires any decorative addition: Its consistent use and suitable processing of the material are sufficient.

Asymmetry is closer to nature than symmetry. Consequently, it is the only order category for a vegetative creation; within the formal-linear design, by contrast, it often seems rigid and static. The colors of an arrangement may also express asymmetry: An asymmetrical subject requires various color volumes.

## Arrangement

The word arrangement designates the expression of a design (see, for example, the school of Weihenstephan). This seems the most appropriate term to describe the different arrangements made possible when handling floral materials and their elements. The three definitions given here – i.e. vegetative, decorative, formal-linear – are controversial even today among different schools of design: While some schools know only two types of arrangement, others name three or even four. These three concepts are most frequently used worldwide and seem to be the most rational since they refer to three totally different motivations of floral design.

While on the one hand, the integrity of flowers and floral materials may easily fall prey to inexperienced or rambunctious creative power, the concept of arrangement provides an exclusive opportunity to experience creativity without boundaries and negative effect. New figures, shapes, even floral sculptures can thus be created, which have never before been seen, if the floral designer does not feel limited by the shape of the floral personality or obliged toward a natural depiction of the flower.

The decorative arrangement is the arrangement most employed worldwide. It is the bread and the butter for most florists. Yet, it should not be the only type of arrangement, otherwise such work may easily become an artistic one-way street. Subordinating the flower to the will of man may also mean the end of aesthetic variety. Nature and the ranking of flower within nature as well as observing floral silhouettes and lines keep all paths open for a lasting creative design.

## Decorative

In professional floral terminology, a decorative arrangement is understood as a rich order of flowers. Traditional, classic floristry usually presents itself as a decorative design.

A further significant feature of the decorative style is the more or less distinct mastery of the floral elements by the hand structuring the same. The outcome of the arrangement is usually an entirely new silhouette, which mostly turns the florals into components claiming only a restrained personality. They submit themselves, are absorbed by a newly created shape – albeit a harmonious shape – and often lose their individuality, depending on whether the silhouette is of ornamental character or rather shows the growth and the lines of the plants. For this, see also the chapter entitled "Grading".

Decorative arrangements have their very own objective: They decorate a room, a corner, and much more. They are taken for granted, are discreet, are able to lift one's spirits, often without the mind consciously being aware of their presence. In the decorative realm, the position of the flower reflects the skilled hand and becomes part of the whole. Different individual colors blend into a new impression of shades. Floral surfaces blend into a new pattern and result in a changed picture with partially surprising effects.

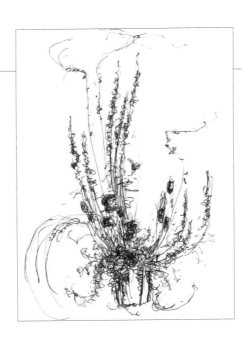

## Vegetative

A vegetative arrangement refers to floristry which concurs with nature as its model. It is synonymous with a naturally grown arrangement of flowers. Structures and lines follow a close natural interpretation. A vegetative arrangement can include featuring individual florals, as well as copying a natural opulent display. Often, entire vegetation communities are depicted in their natural environment: shores, heather, marsh or alpine landscapes.

Vegetative arrangements therefore also require as plain and as natural a container as possible, one which reflects the natural ground in which the floral materials typically grow. The design of the ground significantly supplements the nature-like environment which is to be depicted. A heather landscape has heather soil, an alpine scenery includes stones, faded wood or flat moss. A desert requires sand and stones. Sometimes, the portrayal of such vegetation may pose problems for the florist, if the range of products available in the market is too restricted. Floral designers who can refer to their own garden or to a natural surrounding for their material have great benefit.

A vegetative arrangement always calls for the plant and its elements being used according to their natural growth. Reversals, side winding or other alteration of the materials are not suitable for this type of arrangement.

## Formal-linear

The commonly-used expression is formal-linear arrangement which, however, linguistically speaking, is a slightly inappropriate term and would better be translated as a form-line type of arrangement. Its aim is to express that the silhouette of the floral and its lines are at the forefront of this arrangement. Because this term is one well established in the literature and practice of floristry, it shall be used here as well.

The formal-linear arrangement focuses on the silhouette of lines, flowers, leaves, branches and the assignment of their specific locations, areas, heights, positions – depending on their ideal capability in the interplay with each other. Light florals are emphasized at the top, heavy florals at the bottom; pointed florals to the outside, round to the inside.

Interfering, contrary lines must be carefully observed. This type of arrangement could almost be described as a "ballet of floral silhouette". The arrangement of every line becomes important: Is it active or passive? Intensive studies of silhouettes in the world of flowers are thus indispensable. It is here that one identifies the effect of gathering and releasing, of delicate silhouettes as well as dominant ones. Every silhouette has its place. The varying space between the different materials creates areas of artistic tension. The highestpossible contrast of the material in growth and line underlines the graphic effect of this arrangement. Here, lines never accidentally cross, but instead traverse consciously and intensively so that the effect of any given silhouette is never interrupted but rather emphasized.

A formal-linear arrangement teaches the floral designer to treat flower personalities in a responsible manner by identifying their character in both outline and body and using these observations accordingly. It requires significant detailed knowledge and understanding, as well as much practice, to become a master of this art.

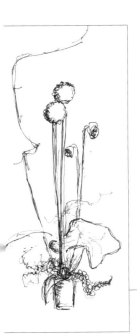

## Arrangement of Lines

The way that the floral lines are arranged is a very important criterion for structuring a floral design. It does not so much describe the flowers, buds and berries, but instead focuses exclusively on stems, long leaves, twigs, branches, long roots, i.e. those linear or bent parts of a plant whose "body" or grain produce dynamics, can determine the direction of design, and draw lines which are presented graphically. The different angle of a line assists with the categorization and depicts variations to the student while imparting new and further possibilities for the experienced floral arranger. The plant's own "activity" of lines – twisted, broken in appearance, seemingly without any order in line, and possibly with a chaos of angles and linear movement – these become the maxim. Although theory can account for the basics, the feeling for how to arrange the lines must be learned.

The natural flow of every single plant, the uniqueness of the individual plant, must be recognized, studied and learned. This requires much practice and many years of development. Managing without the knowledge of nature is unthinkable in floristry.
The various arrangements known to us comprise radial, parallel, diagonal, winding, overlapping and freely-arranged line structures.

This could be extended even further into spiral or broken or horizontal line structures. However, spiral is a cross between "overlapping" and "radial". A horizontal line structure is a rare "special version" mainly used for wall decoration and can also be described as a horizontal-parallel line structure.

## Radial Arrangement of Lines

This term mainly entails the realization that there is a vanishing point from which lines diverge. The lines are, of course, stems or parts of the plant, visible veins, grass, sprigs, flower stalks, etc., which, emanating from this point, run out into the open. Whether these lines are of various length, continue above or even below the horizontal line, is irrelevant. The decisive point is the radius, no matter where it leads to and how far it reaches. The intention is not to import the entire mathematical meaning of the term radial. This will only confuse the student in handling floral materials.

Also, there is no importance in starting with the angle at which the lines leave the vanishing point or the center of growth. This will be determined later by the arrangement and other factors.

A radial arrangement of lines is the most prominently used design. Particularly historic designs are marked by such an order. The architecture of many a plant serves as an example of study (ferns → nephrolepis and phoenix palm tree). The center of growth point can be found by either direct or indirect (imaginary) line structures.

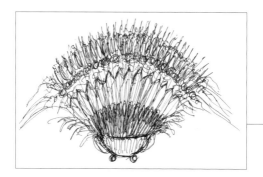

## Parallel Arrangement of Lines

When a flower arrangement clearly creates a parallel line, the result is a certain sense of immobility from which very little positive tension emanates. This static quality does not uplift the onlooker. Consequently, the designer often accentuates the parallel with spontaneous linear, vegetative, overlapping forms of expression. Graphically, the result can be very clear, distinct, and often dramatic. It tends to appeal to a minority. Moreover, it requires a clear adherence to a theme or an ambiance.

Parallel arrangements are subject to a sheer volume of interpretations, provided that the majority of the parts of the plants are arranged upright or the majority of them are parallel to one another. For example: a blade of grass "ascends" at an angle, yet its leaves fall straight down (parallel) such as with pampas grass (Coertaderia). The parallel line structure requires a particularly creative handling with space since it does not – as opposed to radial arrangements – extend or change independently. A parallel structure requires more creativity, with no additional rigid guidelines, to ensure that the floral design will in the end become that special experience. Playing with space already has an entertaining visual effect, and movement within the rigidly straight parts of a plant increases this effect even more, which can further be extended by variable spires.

This calls for conceptional working, based on the rule of a golden section for flowers.
Parallel elements should be placed primarily on the outer boundaries. If the center is emphasized, i.e. raised, it loses its clarity and can appear radial, creating a  triangle or pyramid effect.

The benefit of a parallel design is the possibility of creating eternal lengths or widths of a floral composition with great harmony, and without inadvertently creating the impression of a cut or telescopic arrangement. A parallel arrangement of lines often has the character of a landscape or a garden and is frequently used in this respect.

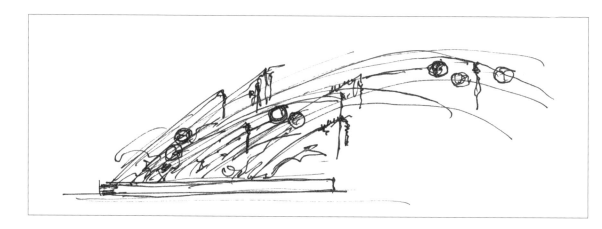

## Diagonal Line Arrangement

This is the "slanting" little brother of the major heading Parallel Arrangement. Not used very often, it describes the inclination of arrangements toward one side which are more or less arranged in diagonal elements. The formal linear realm is graphically interesting, close to nature, vegetative plants bent by the wind, or for the decorative realm of a room or a formal event. Diagonal arrangements can also run in lines parallel to one another, hence the proximity to this issue. Diagonal also means spontaneous, unusual, fresh, detached from any conventional rules, and is a real eye-catcher. It can evade "strong" objects surrounding the arrangement, discreetly making way, yet delicately decorating the scene. The diagonal arrangement may also refer to the structure of textures, but can also be found in anything overhanging boundaries. The variability of the arrangement of lines is rich and exciting as hardly offered by any of the other categories.

## Winding Line Arrangement

A winding line arrangement is more likely to be found in natural than in decorative or linear floral designs unless a decorative structure is created where winding lines overlap with other florals to establish a new entity comprising different floral shapes. It is surely an alluring possibility to depict winding line arrangements. Such a winding effect is most easily created by climbing branches, but also by using various allium and papaver stalks.

This type of line arrangement, however, is to be distinguished from "wrapping", where floral or non-floral materials are manually wrapped tightly around a stick or a stem. The winding line arrangement can ascend or descend or move in a horizontal direction. This version of line flow can also easily be used to accentuate an arrangement or provide a sense of excitement in designs dominated by other line arrangements. An example of this is the parallel design where the eye is surely grateful for a change since otherwise it is not necessarily intrigued by versatility. A broader spectrum of application can be found for vegetative plants where natural scenes are to be created. Yet the question arising here again and again is: Where does the floral designer find inspiration?

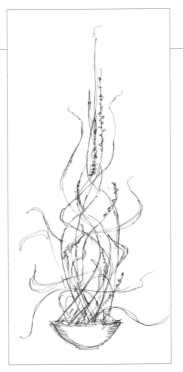

## Overlapping Line Arrangement

Often a very exciting design – when lines of the plants cross, when directional forces flow against one another – when flowers, buds, leaves, etc., literally pour toward a center, partially intertwining, partially by-passing, partially blending in. Such a design usually involves a flat angle of upright, arranged or tied florals. The steeper the angle, the more interesting the graphics of the stems. Particularly alluring is the overlapping effect of the asymmetry. This increases tension. Likewise, this effect is also intensified for stems without foliage or with a very smooth surface and whose leaves or thorns have not been removed manually. For table decoration, they serve as a medium to create exciting arrangements of little space with relatively low height. The handling of potted plants also offers creative assistance to present a fascinating wealth of shapes.

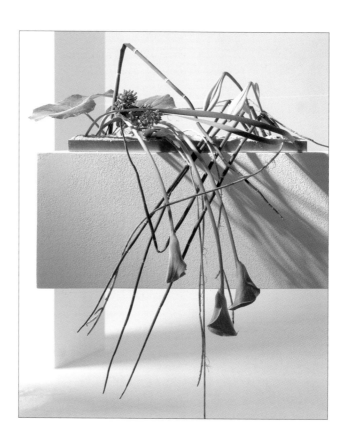

## Free Line Arrangement

A fascinating topic which does not refer to creative anarchy but instead offers the opportunity to sprout floral shapes with great ease over a vast surface, excluding the dynamics created by recurring lines. A lack of line dynamics can either "soften" or create desirable chaos, which is very often requested, if not even sought in graphic or natural motifs.

This type of line arrangement is anything but unprofessional, since only the conscious and skillful ignorance of an "orderly" line structure makes it appear aesthetic and qualified. For example: type of order? type of arrangement? viewpoint ? proportion and definition of structural designing, all need to be attended to. Supposedly the creation of presumed confusion, yet in reality the result of disciplined chaos, it is one of the most current and challenging floral topics of our times. The unstructured line arrangement is also directly related to the position of the focal point. Either it is totally missing here, or the origin of every floral line is described as the anchor. Subordinate line arrangements are ideal for any design, an enrichment to the art of floristry. One should not, however, assume that an arranger will acquire professional floral designing skills merely by tugging and pushing subordinate lines haphazardly into one another!

## Position of the Center of Growth / Focal Point

The various positions that a center of growth can take provide a highly interesting starting point for the floral designer, especially where a vertical arrangement is concerned. While traditional floristry primarily produced a collection of "terminal linear points" in the container, other attractive alternatives have evolved lately. This small chapter is dedicated to the development of artistic alternatives and to their intentional use.

## Center of Growth / Focal Point below the Container

If the lines of the floral materials meet below the top edge of container, there is more space at the top of the arrangement for silhouettes: angles are less pointed and often seem to run parallel. Using this technique, the designer can thus establish generous column-like silhouettes focusing on the center. The position of the center of growth/focal point below the container is also very interesting if the "vegetative" incorporates important lines meeting below the planter, running through the natural ground design in a seemingly effortless manner, literally "going through it". Even if the lines of several arranged groups meet below the planter, a beautiful and natural generosity is created. Such imaginary reference points, however, require training and practice until instinct tells the designer how to handle such elements of design.

## Center of Growth / Focal Point in the Container

The most commonly used version of positioning the center of growth or the focal point is in the container. It is still a very current item. As a rule, radial images are created here, where the top of the arrangement permits only few different florals yet favors more generous individual silhouettes. The assortment in the container is easy and quick to grasp visually, thus presenting the easiest task in this category – if it weren't for the diversity of potential containers. Even for a high slender vase, diversity of shape is significant. This initiates the arrangement of bent stalks to find the way out of the container into the open and down, when dealing with a radial arrangement. Grading (see individual chapter) is a means to play with changes and other degrees of difficulty.

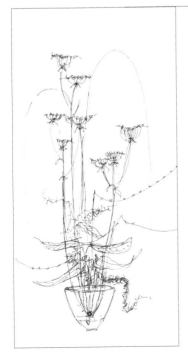

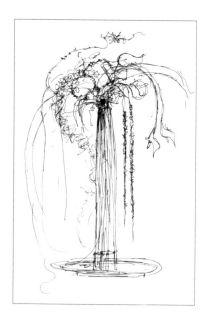

## Center of Growth / Focal Point above the Container

A new and contemporary version is the position of a center of growth above the container: so-called standing bouquets – as termed by customers and the public. Tied, freely standing arrangements are worked around this position of a growth center or focal point. When upright lines (stalks) run to an elevated point where once again they diverge as a line of the entire arrangement, which is the main point of the artistic unit, one attractive possibility in using standing bouquets is to work the multidirectional option downward. However, one difficulty with this kind of work derives from the lack of proximity to the container, which usually provides the floral designer with much orientation in terms of proportions. The customary support is missing as well as the sense of stability. Nonetheless, many people all over the world are fascinated by this design possibility, mainly because standing supports are built – so-called floral superstructures, basic structures, sometimes something that can even be called a frame – which very often are both interesting and fun to work with. However, these supports can also prove very time-consuming at times.

## Center of Growth / Focal Point beside the Container

It is not often that a designer chooses to position the center of growth beside the container. Yet it is an interesting option for sideboard or buffet decorations or also for long, horizontal designs which aim strongly either to the left or to the right. Moreover, this positioning allows elements to flow either to the front or to the back (depending on the view) so that it does not pour out from the outer walls of the container too pointedly. In addition, it allows an imaginary start of the lines outside, behind or in front of the container to establish a broader base. It also prevents pouring arrangements from leaping out of the planter, which would already significantly restrict the choice of material since in such a case, only a few, highly flexible stems and soft climbers or flowers of bent or slanted growth could be used (see sketch).

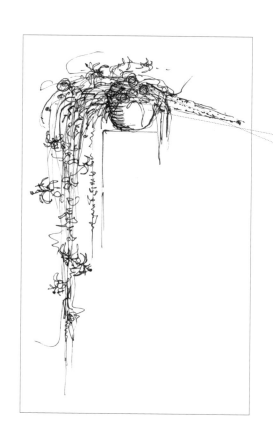

## Number and Arrangement of Centers of Growth / Focal Points

The center of growth designates a point in the vegetative domain from which lines – i.e. floral elements – jointly evolve, from which they practically seem to grow. For a decorative or formal-linear arrangement it is called a focal point. The term starting point is appropriate when talking about the beginning of a line, but not in the radial sense of the word, i.e. when a singular or even several lines do not unite in their direct or imaginary extension – as in parallel lines.

Very often there is the desire to create arrangements comprising more than a single unit to create a richer, more interesting image. In such a case, a combination of evenly or differently dimensional arrangements can be referred to by arranging several points of growth, focus or starting in a horizontal manner.

The distance between the individual arrangements or groups of arrangements, as well as its height, depends on the order category. In symmetry this may refer to equal distances, heights or rhythms, while in asymmetry the rule of the golden section is assumed: 3:5:8 as the best ratio of the group toward one another. More precisely, the distances toward one another must never be the same, a certain floral spire must never repeat itself – or at least not be clearly visible. Of further significance is also the distribution of size in arrangements with several centers of growth or focal points. In this case it is better to replace the word dimension with volume or substance, since every arrangement not only has height and width but also the aspect of material opulence, i.e. substance. These applications depend on the order category.

## One Center of Growth / Focal Point

One of the most frequently used versions for this type of arrangement is that of working around a single center of growth/focal point. This version is usually employed in radial arrangements where the center of growth/focal point attracts all lines or where they all emanate from the same focal point. Even in antiquity, there were many types of arrangements with a focal center like this. Floral arrangements that have a center of growth/focal point are based on the structure of many plants, such as ferns, palm trees, herbaceous perennials, shrubs and many other types of growth whose dynamic growth emanates from a focal center. Humans have become accustomed to this visual habit and are open to anything floral which presents itself in a tousled, more or less extroverted manner. Likewise, opening up to the outside over the edge of the container is considered an element of lightness, a symbol for the powerful growth of floral elements. The movement emanating from this point tends to be at times active, at times passive, at times exuberant or even poignantly aggressive and radiating.

## Several Centers of Growth / Focal Points

Vegetative arrangements have a center of growth. Decorative and formal-linear arrangements can have several focal points from which the lines can be used consciously without intending to create anything close to nature.
Here, the organizing hand is clearly visible which allocates the plant to its location and does not follow natural examples. Focal points can be used in symmetry as well as in asymmetry - and at even or uneven distances from one another. This applies to the width as well as to the depth. Formal-linear arrangements with several focal points require the highest level of concentration – for the selection of the number of arrangements as well as for other design elements.
Certain structures may also have several focal points provided the segments of the arrangements show a certain tendency of lines running toward a center. See also other examples in this book (p 66, 75).

## Several Centers of Growth / Focal Points in Liberal Arrangements

There are only starting points in parallel, diagonal, liberal and overlapping line arrangements – points from which individual lines emanate. There is no joint reference point where all lines meet, but to speak of a lack of order would be inappropriate. A liberal arrangement also expresses decisiveness.

The structures also reflect designs which do not require a center of growth/focal point. The material starts or ends somewhere without a recognizable center. Particularly arrangements with no visible center or joint reference point have marked recent floristry where a liberal line arrangement has often been appreciated. Even if elements of flowers or plants gather into a much proven grouping, the lines need not have a common source.

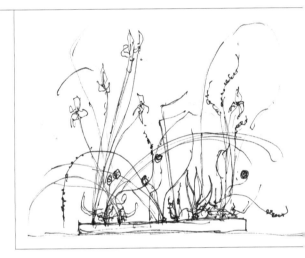

Floral arrangements may very often be characterized by a certain perverse willfulness: specifically, a disregard of proportionate principles as described by the golden section. In floristry, such regularities are applied in the three dimensions of the arrangement, as well as for all directions into which the flowers strive from the focus of the arrangement – up, down, rarely horizontally or diagonally. Particularly for asymmetrical arrangements, the key is the consistency toward clearly designated proportions. Asymmetry is the opposite of regularity, of congruent lengths and proportions. The golden section even assists in the mathematical derivation of asymmetrical proportions.

For humans, proportions are an important, even if at times an unintentional standard of "beauty". They dominate even in nature and determine the aesthetic quality in all human areas of life, particularly in art, architecture and design. Even for filigree, silhouette-like works or their counterpart, i.e. thick, solid designs, the human eye perceives proportions. This is why this decisive factor has its own category in the arrangement guideline.

The golden section provides an easy-to-use tool. Yet practice also brings a certain instinct for harmonious proportions to facilitate a more sophisticated and routine handling of the arrangements. Proportions can be used as a rhythmic, structuring arrangement medium for everything – not only for structures, volumes and expanses, but also, for example, regarding the artistic play with color.

Even the interaction with other creative categories makes proportions a determining factor: In which direction do branches, sprigs, stems go from their center of growth? Which line arrangements and which surfaces dominate? All these are questions which are answered when the arrangement is understood and created as something determined by the proportionate ratio. The knowledge of the right proportion enriches the arrangement spectrum by one of its most elementary and expressive media. Clearly defined proportions not only develop numerous designs – but they also define the logical expressiveness of a floral design.

## Proportions Directed Upward

The vertical expansion is the most popular proportionate design version. It follows elementary principles – first of all the natural semblance of the individual flower, but also the upright figure of man – thus meeting with ancient visual habits. Classic floral works such as pyramid-shaped arrangements and high bouquets very often are proof of upright proportions.

In both the symmetrical or asymmetrical work, the upright proportion brings tension into an arrangement. The crucial point here is that the movement of the floral from its location on the ground, table or stand includes vital dynamics, a striving motion. The line arrangement is only of minor significance here; textures can also embody dynamic upward motion without lines prescribing a perceivable direction. Arrangements of upright proportion suggest grandeur, appear representative, sometimes static, and demand a certain degree of respect from the viewer. They are versatile, though they neither call for a specific order category nor arrangement. The proportions can also be exaggerated or overdrawn here: proportions of length such as 3:6:10, for example, create an exciting and dramatic albeit extreme format, although compacting the arrangement also permits this variety in the arrangement category.

## Proportions Directed Downward

Where proportions are directed downward, the arrangements must be elevated or suspended from the wall or the ceiling. For symmetrical works, there are only two dimensions available for these proportions: Expansion downward must be identical to the width of the arrangement.

In asymmetry, however, the golden section again rules, with the dominating dimension usually directed downward. Naturally, it can also be varied in more extreme proportions (e.g. 3:6:10) or compact arrangements.

In particular when creating an arrangement to be placed on a column, altar, elevated item of furniture, or freely suspended arrangements for wall and interior decoration, falling proportions are used. For most arrangements, the view, focal point or center of growth is located in the upper third of the design, yet this is not a prerequisite. When working with structured or textured structures, for example, it can also have a different position. Density or transparency of material may alter the standard.

## Proportions Directed Horizontally

Here, too, the golden section with its proportionate key of 8:5:3 is a great help, with the dominating horizontal naturally being assigned the highest value. By exceeding the scale, arrangements with horizontal proportions can also achieve impressive effects; elements such as color, density or transparency of the material can all effectively serve as the starting point for such modification.

The horizontal proportion can be set up along the length or side of the arrangement. Additional tension arises from the position of the view, the center of growth or the focal point. It can be placed in a symmetrical or an asymmetrical manner. For structures, this is a subordinate element, yet employing it may prove visually highly attractive.

Arrangements with a horizontal direction are ideal for the decoration of tables, chests, sideboards and surfaces of medium height.

## Proportions Directed Diagonally

Proportions directed diagonally are used so rarely that they are likely to be considered only as a theoretical discipline. Since the basic surface of an arrangement usually also coincides with a "water level", an arrangement can only be made with dry material or by using water reservoirs such as small tubes for a diagonal proportion.

Diagonal proportions can be particularly attractive if they communicate with the architecture of the surroundings and retrace the slanting of a staircase, of a wall or any other detail (see sketch).

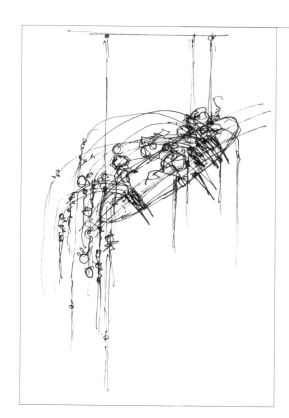

In symmetrical proportions, the expansion of the work in width, height and depth is identical: It evolves evenly around the center of the arrangement into all dimensions. A ball or a cube are such perfectly symmetrical objects. Very classic works of floristry come close to replicating these formats. Arrangements of symmetrical proportions can be implemented with any line arrangement offered by the design; even the different structures can be illustrated. Nonetheless, the regularity of symmetrical proportions lacks tension and therefore other design elements may provide a visual stimulus: color, density, transparency, for example, or simply an exciting combination of materials.

Symmetrical arrangements are typically used as a formal point of contrast in a restless environment; often symmetry also cites the silhouette of the container.

If asymmetry is to be employed, expansion into the physical dimensions must be uneven. The proportions according to the principles of the golden section at 8:5:3 ensure harmony through variation.

## Structural Designing

The term "structural designing" refers to more complexity in the process of arranging flowers, a complexity that requires the designer to exceed the use of basic arranging aids and move into more intricate and time-consuming design practices. The following list of possible design features provides more detailed information regarding this term:

1.) dense compacting
2.) overlapping arrangement (on top and into one another)
3.) tight winding in and around one another and by one another
4.) compiled, set, glued to tight packages or blocks
5.) designed from elements of plants to enhance innate plant aesthetics, using devices
     to hold or guide a blossom or other elements
6.) stacked layers or threading
7.) interwoven or intertwined
8.) bundled

The constant change and expansion of possible aids for structuring arrangements has kept floristry in a creative state over the past years. Naturally, the future will also bring about further new objects and approaches, techniques and ideas.

Structured arrangements require a thorough study of the range and variety of materials available, especially so that the florals do not appear damaged, forced or impaired by man's hand – whereas winding a fiber is naturally a different activity than clinching a leaf or a blossom. Structures employed superficially only may easily seem like a piece of craft. Caution must be exercised to avoid exaggeration: It is the appropriateness and the conformity which counts here – the sensitivity toward the occasion, the persons and many other factors.

Generally, structures are ideal primarily in a decorative order category. Rarely do structured details emphasize arrangements of formal-linear design.

## Structured

Structured arrangements allow the onlooker to enter the interior of the design. Structures designate the inner order of an arrangement, accentuate it and allow it to be comprehensible. The arrangement of the floral elements thereby breaks with visual habits of traditional floristry as embodied by the "extrovert" bouquet opening toward the onlooker like rays of light. Structured designs could therefore be described as "introverted": The design evolves within an allusion to a limiting outer contour. Structures create a sense of the sculptural, of multidimensional motion in the inner free space: a play with shade, depth, and line arrangements, and partially with covered or overlapped segments.

The outer form of the structure must be fairly static to allow a clear definition, so that it can be caught by the eye as the border moves between the inside and the outside. The more vital and exciting the arrangement, the more it can present itself in the free and open space. This formal contrast between the inside and the outside is substantial for the aesthetic of the arrangement as it develops a harmony between peace and activity. By definition, structures cannot be formal-linear, since the formal-linear arrangement uses only few materials. Nonetheless, formal-linear subjects may evoke structures by overlapping and "introverting" line arrangements.

There are more structures to be found in contemporary floristry than at any previous time. In the past it was a taboo to allow the line arrangement of floral elements to cross. As recently as the 60s and 70s, the orientation was geared to formal-linear arrangements. After that, however, structures replaced these design preferences: floral arrangements began to focus on themselves instead of posing in front of the onlooker. Structured arrangements are often designed in an exaggerated manner, sometimes to the point that too much stacked on top causes the florals at the bottom literally to disappear. When arranging structures, blossoms in the limiting space are very often "locked in": Yet what is important, either in terms of color or form, should be allowed to reach the surface of the work – and to be allowed to guide the attention of the onlooker to the inside.

## Textured

Textures occur when materials are tightly linked. A texture is a design technique which brings materials together in order to create a firm, closed surface – set close to one another, without depth, without overlapping. The plant is released from its vegetative context, the artistic will transports it into a new, artificial context. Textures are mainly employed in decorative floristry. The vegetative design with textures is theoretically possible, yet it is rarely used in practice.

The simplest form of textured design combines identical leaves, blossoms or other plant elements so that the surface is similar to that of a carpeted design, without pattern or mixture. Yet the degree of immobility and the structure of compact texture lives only through the different forms of depiction:

1.) The design places the texture or surface of the plant itself into the forefront. In doing so, elements of the plants are either symmetrically or liberally arranged: set, scattered, laid, glued or stuck with floral wire clips.
2.) The plant elements can also be worked to colored or figurative patterns which create a new, surprising look – similar to printed or digital images from individual points of color set close beside one another.
3.) Textured structures also include the intentional design of an ornament. The scope ranges to the representational depiction of objects or scenes. The ornamental arranging within textured structures produces classic motives and formats influenced by religion or folklore suitable for wall or surface decoration. Set in decorative bowls, they can also achieve an original optical effect.
4.) Textures made of florals may also cover shapes of balls, cubes, rods or freely shaped objects.
5.) Textured elements are ideal for further combination – for restless works, their static appearance creates visual points of rest.

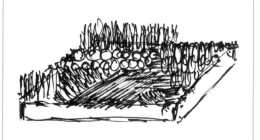

## Designed

These are "edifices" made of sticks, branches, bundled florals and many other materials; tugged into one another, tied, wired, stuck or wound together. A designed structure can be formal, representational or also of free spontaneity. Yet a design with florals requires skills of technique and static equilibrium which have to be systematically acquired so that the arrangement is not shaky or even askew. For this type of structure, the design and the plant elements employed for them are the center of attention, any flower is sparsely used as an emphasis. A clear definition of the volumes of these elements is recommended here: As the base which is more or less covered by florals, any design becomes part of a structure.

Designed arrangements need not be calm, they may also be worked dynamically, taking advantage of space. Yet it would be a lack of imagination for any design to utilize only obvious materials like willow sprigs or bamboo twigs. The wealth of material is seemingly endless. Many options already result from the quality of different florals in terms of stability, load-bearing capacity, flexibility, etc.

Florals can be set in foam, loosely adjusted, wound or woven. There is also the option to equip them with water reservoirs (tubes) made of organic or artificial material – for a free arrangement set within the design, detached from the container.

Designed structures are also feasible without any flowers and foliage: Very often other floral elements are so attractive in terms of color and texture that beautiful and convincing arrangements are created.

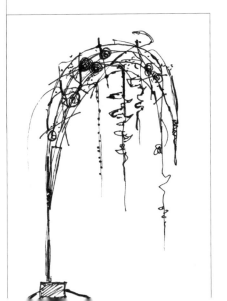

## Object-like

The term "object-like" was used in an individual yet intentional manner by Peter Assmann in his publication entitled Objekte (Donau Verlag). In the broad sense of the term, arrangements defined thereby, such as collages, assemblages, sculptures, open works, can be either of partial or complete floral origin. Many depictions, some very spontaneous, others of deeply-thought articulation, have thus been created over the past 12 to 15 years. The motives are very often of pure artistic or allegoric nature. Their meaning need not always be superficial. These kinds of arrangements very often inspire imagination, make people think, remind them of something, or initiate responses which a work that focuses purely on the aesthetic side does not necessarily evoke. Within the framework of artistic variety, like exhibitions, private views, and presentations, long-lasting versions of the object-like make absolute sense and offer a cultural enrichment for such events. Presentations with plants also develop a certain independence. Object-like arrangements have no clear rules, as do other structures. Spontaneous, impulsive, free expressions here seem obvious and accessible.

## Layered

For this structure, plants and plant elements are layered on top of, next to and beside one another. The possibilities for fixing the same are extremely numerous – florals can be set, laid, wired, threaded, layered, even skewered. The design versions are so versatile that the layered structure allows arrangements of the most various resemblance and effects to be designed.

Threading foliage, blossoms and fruits can be traced far back in time; as early decorative elements they existed even in antiquity, such as in ancient Egypt. They were likewise an integral feature of daily antique culture, such as in pre-Columbian America. Also, in many a contemporary culture, threading is associated with specific plants and kinds of development: Around the Mediterranean, for example, or in Hawaii, spices, fruits and vegetables are threaded as decorative chains.

Layered arrangements should be made from easy to dry or already dried materials. They are ideal for dried floristry and can provide new and unusual impulses, such as with wall arrangements. However, arrangements that use structures, such as densely layered florals, can also be kept relatively fresh through the infusion of moisture into the arrangement.

Layered arrangements also have an effect within a combination: As a compact mass or body, layered structures can compensate and harmonize too restless a floral design.

## Stacked

The phrase "stacked structure" is not quite as common in the German language as it is in the Netherlands or in Belgium. It describes arrangements which are made more or less from a single or only very few florals (not material!) which are designed in a highly creative manner, i.e. using different silhouette and placement options, elaborating on the various sides and views of a floral. A strong limitation of the breadth of a design poses an enormous challenge. The designing hand mainly keeps the possibility of a strict separation of the respective impression through blocks of design – or Mondrianism (Dutch painter and Bauhaus designer, 20s). Such interstacking of the material into different-sized blocks or surfaces is often reminiscent of the layout plan for a building or view of a city. Such a shape is not loose, not natural, yet offers the possibility to work in a modern manner with a lot of material – with florals of the most simple kind which achieve a new effect of unity by stacking or compacting them. This structure mainly makes sense when positioned in a restless surrounding filled with many small items.

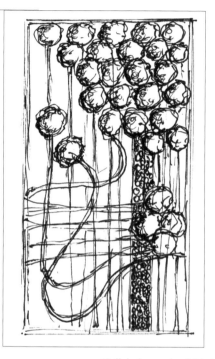

**Wall design made of dried allium.**

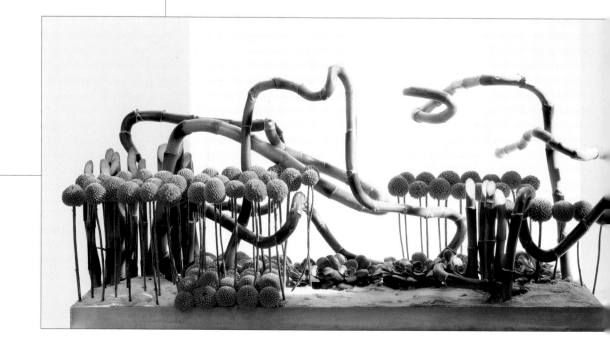

## Winding

Winding arrangements boomed mainly in the 80s. Initially made of purely floral materials, they became increasingly designed with wire, wool, leather ribbons, even in combination with film or metal strips. Yet these structures were overstated and nearly became a mania. After the trend had more or less worn itself out due to such mass production and consumption, it is today returning to the realm of floristry – used in a sensible and moderate way, where a winding structure is aesthetically convincing. Winding structures represent a variety of motives:

1.) to be able to benefit from the authentic and practical functions of the structures – i.e. to attach something.
2.) to procure an altered image of less impressive plant elements like sprigs, branches, tubes by wrapping these into a winding structure, thus exaggerating and emphasizing their visual look.
3.) to add to the natural growth of the plant a visual proof of the arranging hand and thus to project a conscious craft design onto a structure.
4.) to let a blunt tip of a branch or stalk taper into a peaked shape.

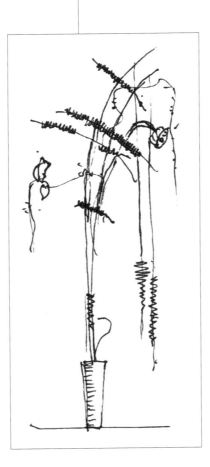

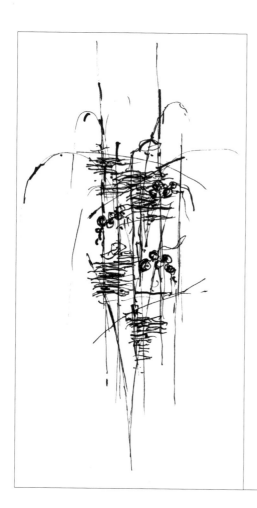

**Braided segments in a hanging surface.**

## Interwoven

As is true with nearly all structures, woven structures also experienced major popularity to the point that they were used excessively. Yet such excesses are very much in the nature of human fascination for new things, for creative challenge.

In the end, the interwoven structure also offers a number of opportunities to make floristry interesting and versatile, to seduce the beholder to take a closer look:

1.) At first there is the possibility to weave or intertwine entire arrangements: fixed to one another or simply loosely interwoven. Fresh, dry or mixed into the material, with or without a water reservoir made of moss, foam pad or tubes made of either glass, zinc or organic substances.

2.) Moreover, interwoven or intertwined segments are mainly used for decorative purposes in other arrangements.

Interwoven or intertwined structures can be used for nearly all areas of floristry and are an attractive invitation to retrace the design with the eye. They enrich interior decoration, wedding and dried floristry, but also the floral designer's daily work with bouquets and arrangements. An interwoven structure is also highly appealing for the floral designer, since the designer has to develop unusual skills with materials that tend to "slide" through the fingers and hands and one must create a design from climbers and fibers seemingly out of thin air.

On a final note, interwoven structures are also a plus for floral collages (Friedhelm Raffel) – here it tends to be a means for compacting, to center the focus onto the material.

## Bundled

A very important design technique. During the years of country-house style, in interior decoration bundled floral arrangements in particular played an important role. Lavender, cereals, cinnamon, willow, cornus, bamboo, equisetum, etc. are well-known materials to be used for this. Bundled structures can focus, arrange, and create calm in restless environment, as well as match spontaneous, wild, restless works. Entire arrangements can be produced from bundled structures, which can be made out of wire, raffia, grapevines, as well as with flexible rods made of willow or other kinds of hardwood switches.

Usually, bundled structures are grouped with arrangements representing a certain country charisma, such as a superimposed bundle of lavender – draped across an opulent arrangement of roses or ivy – to express Mediterranean romanticism by evoking a sense of grapes, herbs and sun.

Bundled structures, however can also be very tectonic and static if they are part of a blocked, textured, stacked, modernized arrangement.

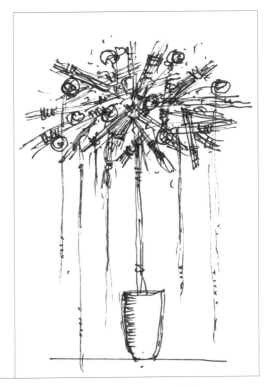

**Bundled structure made of willow with apples in between**

## Grading

Because this book sets classifications, depicts limitations, an explanation may be called for. Classifications and limitations can easily evoke the impression that the design guideline restricts the creativity of the designer. Creating an order guideline, on the contrary, draws attention to the possibilities opened to floral design. Consequently, it may not only be consulted as a working tool and piece of advice before commencing with a design, but may also be referred to for later analysis, i.e. to understand the effective mechanism behind a floral work.

Categorizing, simplifying, bringing a pragmatic and vital order into the discipline – this was never highly respected by some of the most creative arrangers in the industry. The teaching aspect was always scorned in floristry. The image was that of being close to art, representing its freedom as a certain feel for design which had to be acquired, thus keeping new thoughts to oneself. Yet this attitude can hardly coincide with the call for a basic "solid" training. Too much depends on the person of the teacher, since charismatic people who are able to spark and to motivate the student are not so easily found.
Therefore, a complex doctrine is needed which embraces easy to understand basic knowledge and then opens increasingly broad and in-depth dimensions of understanding to the learner, primarily based on logic. Whoever wishes to proceed after this may penetrate the entire complexity of the design guideline, definitions like line arrangements, arrangements, proportions, combining all these and constantly creating new inspiration from this universe of ideas.

Nonetheless, there is still one significant step missing: grading. It is most easily described with the term of a "decorative" arrangement when considered in its entire complex variability. It can appear as a vegetative work as well as with a strong rapport toward a silhouette. Or the parallel design - it may be extremely static, yet moving, may play with heights and distances or even present slightly moving lines and overlappings.
To this extent, all terms of the categorization are variable. Translating the design guideline onto a ball would therefore not be the adequate way to express its multiple directions adequately. It allows for boundless possibilities in design, without sacrificing personal articulation. These options are increased by the variety of materials, by the versions, the shades, the structures and combinations of and with color. Personal development and artistic freedom are not limited by the knowledge of the number and type of possibilities. Whoever nonetheless suspects a dictatorship of doctrine has not understood the nature of "compatibility" in this book. Definitions of grading levels for arrangements are explained with drawings and texts on the following pages.

Grading is simplified by a scale ranging from 1 to 10. 10 respectively is the purest, the most intensive form of the term; 1 the weakest, directed towards the borderline of the neighboring term. To separate grading even more finely, possibly with a scale ranging from 1 to 100, does not make sense: The differences would hardly be perceptible. The design guideline uses the following drawings to best explain the term "grading":

### Level 10

Purely decorative, in the most intensive form: For the ball, green carnations are densely set next to one another onto the polystyro ball, no greenery, flower beside flower. The plant element becomes a component of the entire silhouette.

### Level 9

Initial plant outbreaks are myrtle tips which indicate the most modest starts of growth or silhouette. The first step to the neighboring design is thus already achieved.

### Level 7, for example

The green carnation ball presents a slight graduation as if the blossoms lift and fall in a regular order. Green tuffs and light green climbers "grow" out of and "flow downward".

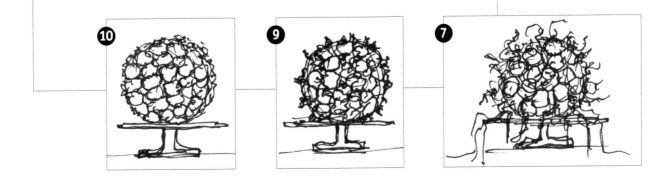

## Level 6

The hermetic shape of the ball dissolves strongly. The arrangement is given a base, the stems of the carnations become visible. Grass, climbers, foliage fill, emerge from and play with the arrangement.

## Level 4

New shapes come together: Freesias join the carnations. The decorative green is also defined more characteristically.

## Level 3

The structure remains symmetrical, the wealth in shape grows. Summer larkspur mark the new design, the inner structure of the work is given a spontaneous, irregular (=asymmetrical) accentuation.

## Level 2

Still decorative, yet by now completely asymmetrical. The volume and lush superstructure determine the presentation – iris, twigs, carnations all ensure contrasts, silhouettes and lines rich in motion which develop with character.

## Level 1

Here is the borderline, the transition to another design category, i.e. formal-linear or vegetative. Any risk here mainly comes from the indecisiveness, the deadly enemy of design until something different is clearly defined and formed on the other side of the border.

**Note:**
As delineated here for the decorative structure as an example, these categories and definitions of the design guideline can be varied. To consider these versions increases individuality of, creativity of and enthusiasm for the design.

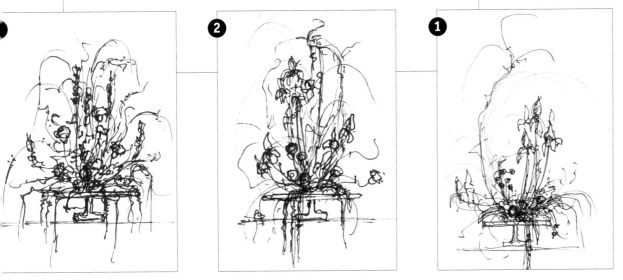

**1: Bordering on the line to a formal-linear structure – the "transition" to the neighboring design**

**Description:**

Here, the parallel-decorative element appears very static – in the photo, it even seems heraldic (like a coat of arms), yet can be used for many an occasion.

**Application:**

Ideal for any wide surface, e.g. as altar decoration, table decoration, adornment for long balustrades. Particularly suitable also for display windows, since the arrangement can be kept at a very low height.

**Technique**

Set in foam.

**Note:**
**Any desired dimensions**
**are feasible for this**
**arrangement. Height,**
**width, depth may all be**
**chosen freely.**

Florals: Nelumbo nucifera, Aloe vera, Crassula obliqua, Rosa-Hybriden, Kochia scoparia, Araucaria araucana, Anthurium-Andreanum-Hybriden, Leucadendron, Philodendron, Echeveria agavoides, Cynara scolymus, Echinacea purpurea, Galax aphylla, Asparagus scandens var. deflexus

**Description:**

Static. Compacted. Like architecture; but also modern and very graphic.

**Application:**

Interesting as a modern table design. Particularly appropriate for table floristry, wall design, since here the ratio between effort and longevity is appropriate and justifies the price.

**Technique:**

Set in foam. Laid. Glued.
A challenge to the craft skills and to artistic creativity.

  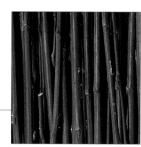

Florals: Aloe vera, Salix caprea, Rosa-Hybriden, Crassula obliqua, Pandanus veitchii

**Description:**

Dynamically aiming for one another, bonding elements which diffuse harmony and tension at the same time. As a symbol of harmony, very expressive and symbolic.

**Application:**

Table decoration or, designed with slightly more height, as a sideboard decoration. Also beautiful as a floral arch placed on columns – e.g. for weddings.

**Technique:**

Set in foam, can be extended as much as liked with water tubes.

**Note:**
The overlapping lines must make sense and result in a comprehensible structure.

 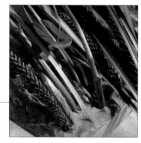

Florals: Araucaria araucana, Ranunculus-Hybriden, Xerophyllum asphodeloides, Bupleurum rotundifolium

**Difficulty: Requires much space in width. Moreover difficult to transport if the setting points are placed in two separated containers.**

**Description:**

Excerpt from nature. Here, a very transparent design. Like
an alliance between the ground and anything that grows;
the creating hand visibly pursues the origin of the plants.

**Application:**

Indoor decoration for informal occasions. Sideboard ornamentation.
Table decoration. Floristry for mourning. As a gift.

**Technique:**

Usually set in foam, whereby the design of the base is usually
adjusted to the respective motif, e.g. water, mountain, rain forest.

**Restriction:**
**Requires a visually calm**
**surrounding to unfold**
**its effect since such a**
**presentation never**
**appears lush, solid, bold.**

Florals: Salix caprea, Galax aphylla, Allium, Thymus vulgaris, Hedera helix

**Difficulty: Very lavish. It is not easy to find good floral winding material at floral supply outlets.**

**Description:**
Like a sculpture. Tight. Tied in. The structure is in the forefront. The plant is dominated by it.

**Application:**
As an arrangement, bouquet, wedding bouquet or floral interior decoration.

**Technique:**
Tied freely on a variety of bases. Such winding structures can also emphasize other arrangements.

**Restriction:**
Work like this rarely seems natural or grown, rather like a craft work.

Florals: Rhipsalis cassytha, Aristea cyanea, Zantedeschia rehmannii

**Description:**

Deliberately restless, creating tension. Slightly disturbing, aggressive. Takes up space. Restricted harmony. Concentration-happy. Contrasting. Hardly flowery. Rather abstract – modern.

**Application:**

As a gift. Arrangements. Table decoration. Collages.

**Technique:**

Tied freely. Set; even for weaving.

**Restriction:**
It is preferable not to use too restless a floral material, but more lines, straws, stalks.

Florals: Ranunculus-Hybriden, Allium, Muehlenbeckia complexa, Salix caprea, Xerophyllum asphodeloides

**Description:**

Delicate; of rich silhouette and contrast. Builds up tension through cross-over.

**Application:**

In a flat, plain dish for table decoration, indoor ornamentation on and in room dividing elements. As a gift.

**Technique:**

Set in foam covered with sand or similar materials. Tied freely on basic floral structure.

**Difficulty: To maintain unity in the arrangement despite variety and contrast.**

Florals: Cymbidium, Zantedeschia aethiopica, Phalaenopsis-Hybriden, Sinarundinaria murielae, Tillandsia usneoides, Rhipsalis-Hybriden, Epidendrum varicosum

**Description:**

Ethnic. Heraldic. Artistic. Bright and sunny. Sophisticated and calm, yet vital, developing dynamically into two dimensions.

**Application:**

Indoor decoration and festive ornamentation for public areas.
Floral focus for symmetrical interior scenes, e.g. in front of a mirror, between columns, etc. To adorn an interior with an ethnic touch.
Can be employed for arrangements, tied freely or in bouquets, even for wedding bouquets.

**Technique:**

Set in foam. Tied freely in basic floral silhouette. Tied to a radial, flat bouquet. Woven as dry wall adornment.

Florals: Echinacea purpurea, Aristea cyanea, Papaver nudicaule

**Description:**

Static. Graphic. Calm. Reduced color scheme in favor of
the effect produced by the highly-contrasting contours.

**Application:**

Table decoration. Indoor decoration for modern, spacious,
calm interiors. As window display. Since dynamics only
evolve upward, also appropriate for display windows and
cabinets. Can be set in an arrangement dish or as a freely
tied work without much height, kept relatively low. Suitable even for small rooms.

**Technique:**

Set in foam, covered with sand. Set in foam
only worked with florals. Set in foam, freely tied
onto a few sprigs or grapevine.

Florals: Alpinia zerumbet, Zantedeschia rehmannii, Kochia scoparia, Ceropegia dichotoma, Phormium tenax, Haworthia truncata,
Asparagus scandens var. deflexus, Salix matsudana 'Tortuosa', Philodendron, Dichorisandra

**Description:**

Modest. Reduced. Delicate and interwoven; placed like a column. Despite visible elements of design through winding and woven elements, still very natural.

**Application:**

As a gift for people with preference for modest, clear style. Accentuated ornamentation for natural-modern interiors. Attractive also as a bouquet. Suitable all year round.

**Technique:**

Set in foam. Tied freely in basic upright silhouette. Also suspended, with tube for water supply.

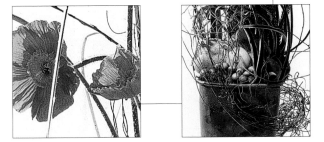

Florals: Xanthorrhoea australis, Equisetum, Papaver nudicaule, Muehlenbeckia complexa, Crassula obliqua

**Description:**

Pillars reaching into the sky. Tight. Dense. Every perspective offers differing views with many details. The guiding hand of the floral arranger can be sensed, for whom plants are essential elements of an entire composition.

**Application:**

Ideal for extremely confined spaces, e.g. reception; as altar or church ornamentation, in front of a pillar, in an alcove, at fair booths of limited space or to accompany architectural silhouettes.

**Technique:**

Set in containers with foam. Can be tied, e.g., into basic cylindrical shape.

Florals: Viburnum opulus 'Sterile', Nelumbo nucifera, Phormium tenax, Vanda Rothschildiana, Philodendron angustisectum, Hyazinthus orientalis, Aristea cyanea, Gentiana, Equisetum palustre

**Description:**

Very symmetrical. Graphic, yet also a little overstated. Appears theoretical, rather symbolic, illustrative, unfloral. Here, consciously exaggerated.

**Application:**

Rarely used; if used, then purely radial to achieve a graphic effect in a modern, symmetrical space. Has a more enhanced effect if completed by structural elements and cross-overs.

**Technique:**

Set in foam. Tied as a bouquet. Suitable as a wedding bouquet to imitate the pattern of the wedding gown.

Florals: Equisetum palustre, Araucaria araucana, Anthurium-Andreanum-Hybriden, Anigozanthos, Rhipsalis, Aeonium holochrysum, Aloe vera, Beaucarnea recurvata, Gomphocarpus fruticosus, Asparagus scandens var. deflexus

**Description:**

Round. Festive. Official. Ornamental. Classic. Lush. Decorative. Permeating. Spreading like rays, adorning. However, also a little plain. Very "present" at first sight, but does not necessarily call for more intensive studies. Corresponds to the "original" floral arrangements of many cultures.

**Application:**

Indoor decoration for classic public areas. Any occasion. Reinforces and underlines, whether festive, gay, sad, official, ceremonial. Set or placed in urns or amphora, baskets, etc.; also as a bouquet.

**Technique:**

Set in foam. Tied as a bouquet. Glued as a collage

**Note:**
This discipline is very often underestimated. Although of plain design, it is very demanding in terms of skill.

Florals: Hyazinthus orientalis, Hedera helix 'Erecta', Galax aphylla, Echinacea purpurea, Rosa-Hybriden, Salix caprea, Typha angustifolia

**Description:**

Rather reduced. Linear. Emphasizes silhouette. Directs the eye to the personality of the plants. Toys with balance, emphasizes and shows different linear processes and arrangements. Benefits from uneven angles; length and height of florals vary: asymmetry is used to fully dominate the system of uneven proportions. The designer explores the floral element according to the motto, "Tell me what you can do for me – then I will work with you". Detachment creates ease. Spaces maintain their effect. The example depicts a radial implementation.

**Application:**

Wherever space or surfaces require more than a decoration or design of quantity. Where an interest in graphics and lines, plant elements and their expression need to be triggered. Also used for a bouquet, an arrangement and or as a small gift where decorative floristry is too costly in vast volumes.

**Technique:**

Set. Tied. Also glued, e.g. for collages.

**Note:**

Formal-linear does not refer to pompous decoration with plants, nor the superficial application of volumes and masses of floras, but the conscious and targeted use of details.

Florals: Alpinia zerumbet, Anthurium-Andreanum-Hybriden, Protea repens, Cortaderia selloana, Epidendrum varicosum, Galax aphylla, Equisetum palustre, Philodendron angustisectum, Nelumbo nucifera

Challenges: Prerequisite is the study and the knowledge of many different contours, lines and variations of plants.

Very demanding on the ability of complex, asymmetrical thinking without compromise and on finding contrasts of silhouettes and lines.

**Description:**

A silhouette is presented as controversial opposing forces.
All dominance enters from one side. Appealing: The eye perceives
tension, opposites become transparent. This work requires a calm
environment to explain itself. The work shown "borders" on the
formal boundary. Graded 2 on a scale from 1–10.

**Application:**

Ideal for a counter or a sideboard. Divider, long living-room
tables. In smaller dimensions, for tables of all kind.

**Technique:**

Set in different media: foam, wire, natural wire, Kenzan, etc.

Florals: Zantedeschia rehmannii, Dichorisandra thyrsiflora, Anigozanthos, Aristea cyanea, Muehlenbeckia complexa, Ranunculus-Hybriden

**Challenge: To clearly elaborate varying proportions, lengths, angles and to create a distance to the focal point.**

**Description:**

Like a silhouette. Transparent. Harmonious cross-overs. Contours are paramount, not so much the illustration of a natural ambiance. Passive downward lines create a calm atmosphere.

**Application:**

Sideboard. Receptions. Visually calm alcove. Cabinet. Exclusively for modern spaces.

**Technique:**

Set in foam. Tied freely. Collages.

Florals: Sinarundinaria murielae, Zantedeschia rehmannii, Kalanchoe blossfeldiana, Tillandsia, Cortaderia selloana, Aloe vera

Challenge: To equally define the balance between asymmetry and contours.

### Description:

Highly decorative and adorning, yet with strong structural rapport: Many silhouettes strive dynamically toward the sky, the semi-circular line softens its slightly aggressive touch. The strong center axis emphasizes the static design at length.

### Application:

Long-lasting decorative indoor adornment, preferably in contemporary ambiance.

### Technique:

Set in foam. Tied. Placed in vase, etc.

### Challenge:

Reinforcing the florals beyond the formal-linear minimum of one, two, no more than three structures.

Florals: Heliconia caribaea, Nelumbo nucifera, Cymbidium-Hybriden, Anthurium, Tillandsia, Aloe vera, Celastrus orbiculatus, Strelitzia reginae, Phormium tenax, Moluccella laevis, Cortaderia selloana

Florals: Papaver nudicaule, Bergenia cordifolia, Hydrangea petiolaris, Hedera helix 'Erecta'

**Description:**

Natural. Growing from a single point. As if dancing in the wind.
Harmonious. Filigree. Unobtrusive. Not forced, yet with a
discreet will for order. Not imposing on the surrounding space.
With tenuous structural rapport.

**Application:**

Adornment for a naturally-designed ambiance with natural
materials and furniture where there are no dominant structures or
textures. Rather for private, intimate occasions, nothing official.

**Technique:**

Not so much tied as set. Design of bottom and base oriented
toward natural ground.

**Description:**

Radial. Gathered at center. Layered. Craft-like. Closed, concentrated. Directed toward a flowering focus, visual focal point.

**Technique:**

Set in foam. Gathered. Tied. Glued. Laid.

**Challenge: Every element taken into your hand is different; therefore gathering natural products (here, willow) is a question of practice.**

Florals: Salix purpurea 'Gracilis', Mahonia aquifolium, Muscari botryoides

**Description:**

Natural. Spontaneous. Very close to nature. Seems highly unmodified, not manipulated. Honest. A long flat item of spring of the south of Europe. Mild, yet controlled.

**Application:**

(Long) Sideboard. On a divider. Also for table decoration. As decoration for display windows, but slightly larger, with water reservoir.

**Technique:**

Set, usually in foam. Tied freely on grapevine base, raffia, wax rope.

**Note:**

Even with a free line arrangement, there are some groups which show a mutual direction; or the same flower (such as here, the tulip) converge from various points of placement as a group in the end.

Florals: Muscari botryoides, Agapanthus orientalis, Tulipa gesneriana, Xerophyllum asphodeloides, Euphorbia, Epimedium versicolor, Cornus sericea

**Description:**

Significant. Symbolic. Powerful. Structural. Framing. Dominating. Artificial skills. Strong. Radial toward the lower part of the composition.

**Application:**

Indoor decoration. Frequently recognizable of similar design, since highly decorative despite strong structural rapport.

**Technique:**

Set in foam. Tied freely on grapevine, raffia. Set in different wire bases.

**Note:**
The point is to observe the proportion of the "ornament" to the entire volume of florals.

Florals:
Xanthorrhoea australis,
Zantedeschia rehmannii,
Fritillaria imperialis,
Sandersonia aurantiaca,
Phormium tenax,
Clematis vitalba,
Sedum nussbaumerianum

**Description:**

Persuaded by the weather into a direction. Seems to have imitated the natural surrounding of amaryllis. Very delicate and conscious illustration of flowers.

**Application:**

Indoor decoration for intimate, private occasions. For an effect beyond the occasion of an important day. Evolving. In pursuit of a cycle of change and fading.

**Technique:**

Set in foam with respective design of base.

**Note:**

A diagonal structure may emanate from a focal point, but may also have several starting points.

Florals: Hippeastrum vittatum, Salix matsudana 'Tortuosa', Hedera helix 'Canariense', Hedera helix 'Erecta', Ranunculus-Hybriden, Aristea cyanea

Florals: Equisetum palustre, Echinacea purpurea, Zantedeschia rehmannii, Phormium tenax, Echeveria

**Note:**

**Diagonal arrangements cannot always be positioned freely in the room. Very often an architectural element (here the wall to the left) is required to establish a credible "visual equilibrium".**

**Description:**

Parade. Pointing into a direction with dynamics, inclined. Display of mutual strength. Exciting. Tense. Surprising, breaking new visual grounds. Lush and clear.

**Application:**

To underline architecture of similar grace: Art Deco and modern spaces. As indoor decoration. Also for a special occasion. Either positioned centrally, but also in front of walls.

**Technique:**

Set in foam. Tied freely in basic floral structure on wire base and other types of mesh. Glued as wall collage.

**Description:**

Growing. Grown. Trailing elegance. Covering sections of the wall. Floral, overflowing. Lasting. Perpetual. Can be adjusted harmoniously since pure flora does not raise any questions of style regarding decoration or formal-linear design.

**Application:**

Grown and set arrangements with cut flowers and plants in modern environment. Usually arranged on a slightly elevated element or on a raised window sill and positioned with absolute front view: altars, etc.

**Technique:**

Set. Grown.

**Note:**

**The trailing silhouette, the proportions directed downward require selected florals which can liberally adorn the naturally-grown structure.**

Florals: Sedum morganianum, Selenicereus grandiflorus, Rhipsalis cassytha, Kalanchoe-Hybriden, Echeveria 'Nürnberg', Graptopetalum paragayense

Florals: Muscari botryoides, Equisetum (dry), Xerophyllum asphodeloides, Pinus nigra

**Description:**

Delicately woven. Horizontally suspended. Light. Filigree. Threaded with flowers. Transparent. Not imposed or "processed". Carried by strong yet thin bars.

**Application:**

As table decoration. Also for a long, modern table where the decoration gives rise to a small item of conversation.

**Technique:**

Set. Setting substance covered with sand. Tied freely, interwoven. Also bound with raffia and glued with various aids.

**Note:**

Woven structures can be very versatile, which is why new paths should always be sought. Each floral is also the matter of a small personal discovery.

**Description:**

Framed, seized in a slightly static manner. Designed into a contour, yet free and vivid. Upright, raised. A flying carpet.

**Application:**

As table decoration. On a sideboard as adornment. As ornamentation for a cabinet because of its restricted boundaries. The carrying effect is ideal for combining flowers, fruits, pods, roots of various florals.

**Technique:**

Set. Tied to grapevine base. Placed indoors. Tied in. The photo: Set in foam, base covered with sand.

**Note:**

When designing a structure it is important that the blooms of the florals extend a little through the wire – i.e. that they reach the surface and do not seem forced into a cage.

Florals: Rosa-Hybriden, Muscari botryoides, Anemone hybridum, Jasminum officinale, Reseda odorata

Florals: Zantedeschia aethiopica, Polygonatum, Anthurium-Andreanum-Hybriden, Dichorisandra thyrsiflora, Jasminium officinale, Vanda, Ammi majus, Asparagus retrofactus, Viburnum opulus 'Sterile'

**Description:**

Raised. Lifted. Stems redesigned as stands. Lightness.
Surprising due to the unusual, clearly visible point of balance.
Exciting. Unconventional. Yet purely organic.
Organically grown nature.

**Application:**

As sideboard decoration. As decoration on a display table.

**Technique:**

Usually tied freely as a so-called free-standing bouquet with different
base techniques (see Lersch: Standing Ovations). But also set in foam
or Kenzan. To extend the stems, additional water-retaining natural
stalks can be used, but also glass or zinc tubes.

**Note:**
The technical steps
required to make
these arrangements
necessitate great know-
ledge and inspiration,
and need much practice
and experience.

**Note:**

To modulate an imaginary anchor of growth or vanishing point (also called meeting point) offers an interesting opportunity to develop further dimensions of one's creativity. The floral designer develops a wealth of variations in the design of basic floristry structures.

**Description:**

"Semi" parallel shooting stems inclined only slightly to the inside as if aiming toward a point as vanishing anchor located below the dish. Using such an imaginary deep point allows for more physical expansion at the top.

**Application:**

More for decoration purposes. Not necessarily limited to confining, even layers. Graded layers are also possible. For indoor decoration, a vase, grown work. Also used often in the vegetative realm.

**Technique:**

Usually set in foam. But also tied freely on wire base and Kenzan.

Floals: Dracaena fragrans, Ornithogalum arabicum, Cornus mas, Tillandsia xerographica, Asparagus scandens var. deflexus, Ranunculus-Hybriden, Rhipsalis capilliformis, Hedera helix 'Eanariense'

**Description:**

Wild. Free. Very close to nature. The organizing hand
of the floral arranger is not perceptible.
Interwoven, winding thicket and interwoven creeper
dominate the scene.

**Application:**

Vivid floral counterpoint in a static ambiance.

**Technique:**

Set in foam, wire base, mesh, tied as a bouquet or for
a wedding bouquet. Tied freely with grapevine, raffia. etc.

**Note:**

Winding is a manual
process. The formation
shown in the picture as
opposed to this, emanates
from the growth and the
design of the individual
parts of the plant.

Florals: Bulbinella hookeri, Salix matsudana 'Tortuosa', Papaver nudicaule, Anethum, Hedera helix,
Aeonium holochrysum

Florals: Rhipsalis, Protea, Phalaenopsis-Hybriden,
Zantedeschia rehmannii, Echinacea purpurea, Tulipa gesneriana, Graptopetalum paraguayense, Kalanchoe

**Note:**
Formal-linear has particular stimulus when of elongated and low design. Not too many florals should rest on the base, instead the structure should carry itself at a little distance.

**Description:**
Low. Elongated. Exciting: the contrast between areas of extreme concentration and great ease. Appears lasting, perpetual, resistant but also sophisticated. Superelevates and idolizes nature as an object, an "item". Reminiscent of sculptures.

**Application:**
In dishes for floral arrangement. As a gift. As indoor decoration of longer-lasting ornamental value. As table decoration: however not for laid dinner tables, more for living-room tables and then arranged within flat asymmetry.

**Technique:**
Set in foam. Root wired with two, three strong wires (0.18 cm) through drilled holes so that several forks are created.

**Description:**

Wide. Rhythmic. Simultaneously seems like both an entity and three arrangements of different heights. The sections refer to one another – however only relatively: volumes, spires, angles vary greatly. Only the "main axes" have a joint meeting point far below the base.

**Application:**

Ideal for a wall protrusion. Fireplace. Mantelpiece. Sideboard. Stage apron.

**Technique:**

Set in foam. Tied freely in elongated dishes. Placed in various-sized individual containers.

**Note:**

**The expansion and volume of the individual elements of a group vary greatly in their asymmetry.**

Florals: Orthophytum, Anigozanthos-Hybriden, Zantedeschia rehmannii, Salix matsudana 'Tortuosa', Anthurium-Andreanum-Hybriden, Beaucarnea recurvata, Epiphyllum anguligerum, Ranunculus-Hybriden, Rosa-Hybriden

**Description:**

Floating. Raised. Lush. Yet a singular upward flow. Not so much romantic, rather decorative, modern.

**Application:**

Table decoration for a larger round or elongated table. Decoration for rooms in which there are many people. Buffet decoration.

**Technique:**

Raise and fix loose wreath of climbers on sticks in foam. Flowers with long stems reach foam bottom. Shorter flowers are in organic (floral) water tank or glass or zinc tube.

Florals: Fritillaria imperialis, Tulipa-Hybriden, Viburnum opulus 'Sterile', Citrus, Lunaria annua, Rosa-Hybriden

**Description:**

Relatively liberal. Hardly structured. Spontaneous, released from conventional basic rules. Creative.

**Application:**

As a bouquet for counters. On a column. Indoor decoration but not for a particular occasion. Nothing official.

**Technique:**

Set in foam or wire base. Arranged liberally in a vase or planter. Tied freely with grapevine or raffia. Placed in flat container.

Florals: Papaver nudicaule, Asparagus asparagoides, Gentiana, Asparagus retrofractus, Tulipa-Hybriden, Tamarix, Beaucarnea recurvata, Salix matsudana 'Tortuosa', Equisetum palustre

**Note:**
Parallel formations like this one are on the borderline to a "texture", nearly creating the transition. This underlines the necessity of grading the individual categories of the guideline.

**Description:**
Purist structure in Spain thanks to Enrique de Leon – very widespread contrast. Dynamic elements (aristea foliage) order the arrangement.

**Application:**
As table decoration, such as for a conference, or for dry floristry in a wall frieze.

**Technique:**
Usually set in foam. Set in flat containers, on wood. Glued.

Florals: Equisetum palustre, Aeonium holochrysum, Galax aphylla, Rosa-Hybriden, Aristea cyanea, Rudbeckia echinacea, Salix sachalinensis 'Sekka'

**Description:**

Stately. Floating. Light. Interwoven, yet not too much (see grading). Simple, plain. Transparent. Modern. Not outright romantic.

**Application:**

For indoor decoration. On a sideboard. On a dresser. In a flat bowl, planter, vase or on a stand.

**Technique:**

Raised with water tubes. Work basic formation from sprigs. Set in foam. Or tied freely to various "base structures", stones or wood.

**Note:**

**The "woven" and "designed" formations are very similar. Particularly the variety of options is fascinating in creative design, yet never neglect the actual objective.**

Florals: Papaver nudicaule, Muehlenbeckia complexa, Euonymus europaea, Passiflora caerulea

Florals: Bulbinella hookeri, Aspidistra lurida, Oncidium varicosum, Cornus mas

**Note:**
It is not possible to sustain something "vegetative" in a daily routine without compromise. The orthodox division into floral realms is difficult. To combine what can grow together is sufficient for environments from a pragmatic point of view, yet does not replace the science of botanic correlation.

**Description:**
Delicately bent by the wind. Swaying with the wind. Recognizing the rules and state of nature. Not representative. Discreet, still. Discovered by accident.

**Application:**
Indoor decoration, rather for public than for private areas. Foyer decoration, e.g. in office buildings. Table decoration for settees. Parapet in modern spaces.

**Technique:**
Set in foam, covered with something organic like sand, stones, moss.

**Description:**

At first sight slightly static, bizarre. "Pure beauty" does not seem to
be at the forefront; instead the creative variation of only two or
three florals appears mainly through the option of a silhouette.
A challenge for florists used to a variety of shapes and colors:
"Floristry for Designers" – (Floristik für Formgeber) by Boletzky.

**Application:**

For a modern space for onlookers familiar with trends. For set arrangements
in the "limelight" to present florals in a spectacular manner.

**Technique:**

Set in foam. Gathered also possible. Tied freely with grapevine or raffia.

**Note:**

**Stacking is greatly linked
with reducing variety
(origin: Netherlands, 60s
and 70s). When prac-
ticing with only one or
two floral materials, this
design guideline helps
extend the spectrum of
variations.**

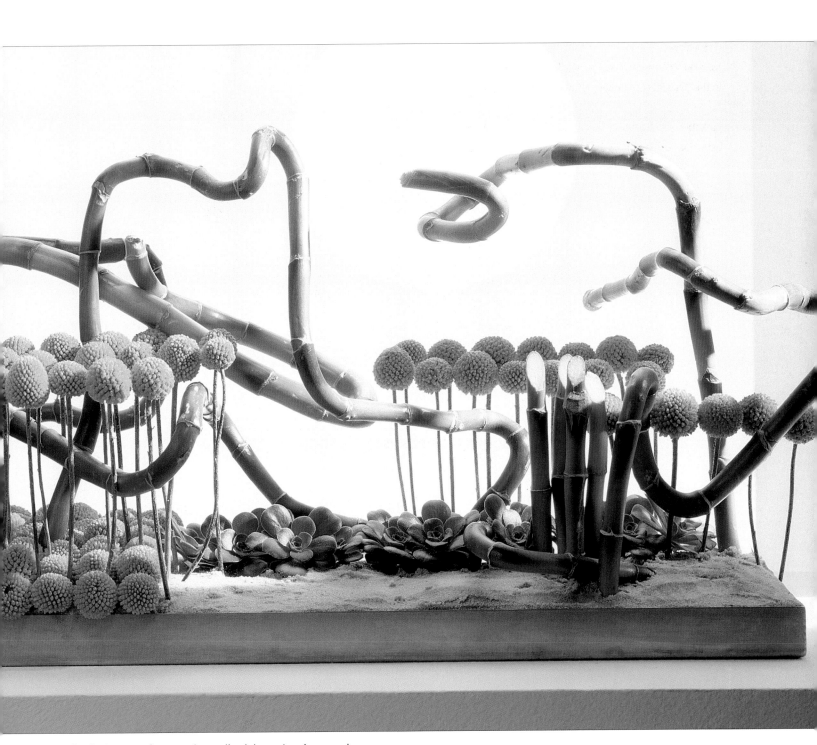

Florals: Dracaena fragrans, Craspedia globosa, Aeonium manriqueorum

**Description:**

A gallery of formations. As if only just placed there. It is only the silhouette that counts; the line, too, but only secondarily. Each element has its own place.

**Application:**

Indoor decoration and divider. Reception area, reception counters. In front of displays. Entrance halls.

**Technique:**

Set in foam or Kenzan. Tied with grapevine and raffia.

Florals: Phyllostachys spec., Hippeastrum vittatum, Anthurium-Andreanum-Hybriden, Araucaria araucana, Dracaena marginata 'Tricolor', Aeonium haworthii, Aloe div.

**Description:**

Carefully designed and crafted. As if made to support the florals, hence the first impression. But also asymmetrical and dynamic.

**Application:**

Can be used for the most various positions: placed, hung, suspended. An interesting object which initiates communication.

**Technique:**

Tied freely with grapevine or raffia. Then set in foam or as a standing, tied formation in water-filled container. Also with water reservoir (glass or zinc tubes) on stone.

**Note:**

This formation demonstrates a relatively young field of design, which opens many possibilities. The important thing is to decide if the basis or liberal florals are to dominate in volume (see formation).

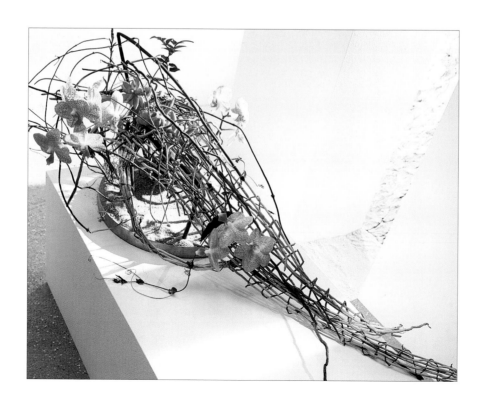

Florals: Vanda Rothschildiana, Sedum nussbaumerianum, Haworthia fasciata, Jasminum officinale

**Note:**

Winding arrangements are fun to design. But here, too, the decision is whether the structure or the unmodified floral is to dominate the formation (e.g. 3:8, 8:3).

**Description:**

Recognizable formations. The hand of the floral designer has reshaped the plant itself. Like an ornament from nature. When winding florals, the accent lies with such plant segments as sticks, sprigs, roots, long leaves. This clearly shows the purpose of fastening and tying in an arrangement, translating it into an aesthetic function.

**Application:**

For all areas. This formation can be used in many ways, except for vegetative arrangements where only floral growths are shown in their ambiance.

**Technique:**

Winding bindweed, jasmine, clematis creepers. For more decorative elements also wire, rope, wool, leather.

Florals: Zantedeschia rehmannii, Jasminum officinale, Echeveria agavoides, Equisetum palustre

**Description:**

Surface emphasized. Strict. Dense. Ornamental. Dominating pattern. Accentuates the geometrical but also the non-geometrical formation. Nonetheless, a central meeting point can be assumed.

**Application:**

Wall tableau. A ball or other body made of fresh or dried flowers. Flat table decoration.

**Technique:**

Glued onto various bases. Set in foam. Layered. Placed (see F.J. Wein). Gathered and wedged.

**Note:**
**Textures on firm bodies are ideal formations with a visual distinction when used in a restless environment.**

Florals: Xerophyllum asphodeloides, Rosa-Hybriden, Echinacea purpurea, Equisetum palustre, Lunaria annua

**Description:**

Attractive. Calls for a comprehensive inspection. Designed toward the center. Floral focus on the surface and inside the weaving. Not only of radial or parallel arrangement: The materials lie, stand, flow into all dimensions. Certain parts of the plant cover one another when viewed from a specific perspective.

**Application:**

For all areas. Because nature itself also structures, even a vegetative design will permit certain structural elements, even if they are never of stylized design or let the craft become visible.

**Technique:**

Tied. Set in foam. Worked with floral base. Grown also possible. Various materials can be used, from fresh to dry florals.

Florals: Calendula officinalis, Sandersonia aurantiaca, Equisetum palustre, Echeveria agavoides, Aristea cyanea

**Description:**

Like a cascade. Soft. Flowing. Leaping over the edge, then falling steeply.
As if lightly grown into and above one another, evenly loosening when falling.

**Application:**

Decoration for a fireplace, mantelpiece, altar. On a gallery, stage apron.
On high furniture.

**Technique:**

Usually set in foam. Set in containers with mesh. Also tied freely into basic
structure with grapevine or raffia.

**Note:**

Observe that the majority
of trailing lines are
truly vertical and parallel,
to ensure the flow.

Florals: Equisetum palustre, Jasminum officinale, Zantedeschia rehmannii, Gloriosa Rothschildiana,
Hoya linearis, Euonymus europaeus

Note:
The formation is tapered towards the bottom so as not to divert from the focal point positioned in the upper third.

**Description:**

An arresting contour. But not only the collective basis counts, the respective flowers remain formal individuals. Decorative, yet with a clear association to the different elements of the flower. The arrangement to the inside via superimposed parts of the plant provide depth.

**Application:**

On a column or a stand. On an elevated piece of furniture. As decoration for an altar. As a bouquet. As a wedding bouquet.

**Technique:**

Tied in a bouquet. Set in foam. Set in mesh.

Florals: Monstera deliciosa, Dracaena fragrans, Sandersonia aurantiaca, Equisetum palustre, Echeveria agavoides, Aristea cyanea, Gomphocarpus fruticosus

**Note:**

Here the accent of the color defines the focal point: The white calla dominates in volume, yet in contrast to the yellow base, these are clearly in the background.

**Description:**

In motion. Lush. Exotic. With a variety of shapes over and next to one another. The decorative order is ranked at the bottom end of the scale. One formation is particularly obvious: structural. Line arrangements therefore play an important role.

**Application:**

On a column, a cube, an elevated piece of furniture. Not necessarily for a front view, but more from the side. Also on a filigree stand as a decoration in front of or by a lectern.

**Technique:**

Set in foam. Tied as a bouquet into basic structure. Liberally tied in basic structure, standing on a flat container.

Florals: Strelitzia reginae, Solanum, Asparagus scandens var. deflexus, Zantedeschia aethiopica, Vanda Rothschildiana, Asclepias physocarpa, Anthurium-Andreanum-Hybriden, Equisetum palustre, Asclepias fruticosa, Leucospermum cordifolium

**Description:**

Filigree. Loving, playful, plain, trailing. Spring-like, delicate. Romantic, despite a rather cool environment. With a light country-house touch. Popular in central and north Europe.

**Application:**

In romantic, cozy environment. To match the country-house style: rural dresses, lace sets, old furniture of simple motif. As a tied bouquet or a wedding bouquet. As a small arrangement.

**Technique:**

Placed in a vase. Set in mesh. Tied as a bouquet, set in foam: Leave foam slightly above the rim of the container and let delicate, flexible material trail over edge.

**Note:**
**The focal point of this formation faces toward the onlooker at an angle of approximately 45°.**

Florals:
Viola wittrockiana,
Tulipa-Hybriden,
Muscari botryoides,
Jasminium officinale,
Tillandsia usneoides

Florals: Anthurium-Andreanum-Hybriden, Echeveria agavoides, Hyazinthus orientalis, Eremurus bungei, Hippeastrum vittatum, Tulipa gesneriana, Dracaena marginata 'Tricolor', Viburnum opulus 'Sterile', Cornus mas

**Description:**

Very radial. Opening to all sides. Converging in the container.

**Application:**

As a gift. Indoor decoration in a planter or dish. Layered, tied bouquets.

**Technique:**

Set in foam. Tied to a bouquet with raffia.

**Note:**

Even the same arrangement reveals many variations by setting the focal point at different heights.

**Note:**
Textures generally tend to be categorized as structures. This composition however appears very natural – even though it depicts an arranged surface.

**Description:**

Mountainous florals, tamed by the weather, like carpet creepers, lichen, moss. Modest. Content. Intimate, not crossed over. Close to the ground. Close to life. Natural.

**Application:**

Surface arrangements for the floor or for a table. The flattest design available for table decoration. "Academic" work, rarely used in practice.

**Technique:**

Laid. Grown in substrate. Stuck by clinging on moist foam.

Florals: Geum borisii, Viola cornuta, Euonymus radicans

**Description:**

Layered. Winding. The structures dominate. Elements of the plant
are processed, modified. New structures are created.
Very skillful appearance, the working process is visible.

**Application:**

Versatile areas of application. Important aid to accentuate decorative
floristry: Layering flowers, foliage, fruits, seeds, bark, chains of pods
to accentuate focal points, for frames, etc.

**Technique:**

Gathered. Layered. Drilling holes, piercing, threading segments.

**Note:**
To produce an entire
formation from layered,
threaded or skewered
elements is rather
unusual and is rather a
part of floral craft work.
In dry floristry, maybe
also for wedding
bouquets, however,
this type of work can be
extremely attractive.

Florals: Lunaria annua, Papaver nudicaule, Jasminum officinale, Echeveria agavoides

**Note:**

Since the plants of various floral realms have been gathered here mainly based on the criterion of color, the German viewpoint is that it is decorative. However, in the south of Japan for example, all these plants grow in a single environment. Therefore, the design of the vegetative, the common botanical origin can only serve as a general guideline: Those which can grow together can also be combined.

**Description:**

Wound like a thicket, even if such effects like bent or gathered flowers have been included. A color theme is recognizable. Ranked in the bottom part of the scale for decorative elements, close to the vegetative (2–3). Like a scenery.

**Application:**

As a divider or a screen with colored focus. To structure a stage.

**Technique:**

Set in foam, base covered with sand, moss or foliage. Tied freely with grapevine or raffia. Firm sticks or sprigs (here willow) as supporting formation.

Florals: Tulipa-Hybriden, Hyazinthus orientalis, Hippeastrum vittatum, Salix caprea, Taiwan "silk", Eukalypthus gunnii, Echeveria agavoides, Anigozanthos-Hybriden, Viburnum opulus 'Sterile'

**Description:**

Light. Reduced to the bare necessity. Evolving from a single anchor. Silhouette and lines
in contrast, yet clearly separated from one another. Every part of the plant has its own
domain. The majority of the design trails. Mathematical proportion: three up, five to the
side and eight down.

**Application:**

As an arrangement. As a hand bouquet or a wedding bouquet with natural stems. As emphasis
in a private room: on a shelf, sideboard or cabinet.

**Technique:**

Set in foam or Kenzan. Tied with raffia or wired and taped. Wedding bouquet with moss
(see Weihenstephan).

Florals: Hoya linearis, Dracaena fragrans, Billbergia nutans, Anthurium-Andreanum-Hybriden,
Asparagus asparagoides, Aristea cyanea, Euonymus europ., Hedera helix 'Canariense'

Florals: Hypericum calycinum, Crassula argentea, Hydrangea petiolaris, Eucalyptus gunnii

**Description:**

Regular round body of uneven surface design. Yet clear type of order. The shape of the body dominates, the floral surface is its decorative "frock". The structure and thus the hand of the floral arranger is visible.

**Application:**

As floral accessory to a home. As wall or ceiling decoration, usually dried or drying. Clever designs as ideas for a gift. A Christmas decoration accessory.

**Technique:**

Set. Glued. Laid. Stuck. Wound.

**Note:**
A grading can also apply within the realm of textures – there are transitions to many other definitions, such as towards the structural or the natural. Grading thus triggers a versatility of design.

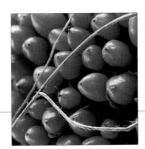

**Note:**

A design need not look rigid.
Flowers may lead the design
or may be led by the same.

## Description:

Like a tower in scaffold. Worked into a construction. Liberal floral shapes tamed in a tectonic space. Flowers look as if in a cage, but visibly extend beyond the boundary.

## Application:

Because of a good formal separation, ideal against a restless background, such as an indoor decoration for a vivid interior. Decoration for a buffet. For a reception or for tables in conference rooms or in the reception area. Against a living still scenery if used outside.

## Technique:

Set in foam. Tied freely with wrapped flowers placed in a bowl with water. Design the water surface with water lenses or the ground with sand and stones.

Florals: Equisetum, Equisetum palustre, Viburnum opulus 'Sterile', Tulipa-Hybriden, Narcissus tazetta

**Description:**

A weave. A floral network. Flowers delicately embraced, suspended freely. Light. Transparent. Floral and textile of surprising combination (ratio 8:3). A structure of substantial natural appeal.

**Application:**

For merchandising. In shops and at exhibitions. As decoration by a lectern. As altar decoration for weddings. As stage adornment. Or permanent decoration as wall carpet in dried floristry.

**Technique:**

Braiding. Tied with raffia or grapevine, with natural tube or glass tubes as water reservoir. Dried with flowers, seeds, capsula, flowers etc. either woven in or glued on or in.

**Note:**

A woven design enables an arrangement of very low height while simultaneously bringing a strong charisma forward. Using a range of water containers has revolutionized the possibilities of this structure.

Florals: Phalaenopsis-Hybriden, Aristea cyanea, Chrysalidocarpus lutescens, Viburnum opulus 'Sterile', Vanda Rothschildiana

**Description:**

Structure on top of structure. The personality of the plant in a dynamic dance with the most various angles and directions of movement. Alliance of the particular. The imaginary intersection of the lines is below the rim of the container.

**Application:**

As a gift in a dish, planter, vase. As a bouquet or wedding bouquet.

**Technique:**

Set in foam or mesh. Tied to a bouquet. Tied as a wedding bouquet with natural stems or wire technique (+ tape).

**Note:**
The possibility to position the meeting point deep inside the container expands the spectrum of arrangement, creating the possibility of a targeted development of tension: A strong center releases spots of reduced structures into other dimensions (here: to the side, back).

Florals: Zantedeschia rehmannii, Heliconia caribea, Kalanchoe tubiflora, Epiphyllum anguligerum, Beaucarnea recurvata, Strelitzia reginae, Zygopetalon brachypetalum

**Note:**

Prerequisite for a formal linear work is the precise knowledge of shape and its principles. For trailing work, this applies even more so. At the same time very demanding in terms of skills and feel for the options provided by a floral material.

**Description:**

Like snakes winding their way over a cliff downward. No active motion, but passively exposed to gravity. Structures and lines in the open space. In a parallel trailing flow.

**Application:**

Indoor decoration in modern spaces of calm design. Resting on elevated furniture or on a mantelpiece.

**Technique:**

Set in foam. Tied to basic floral structure, placed in dish with water. Flowers with soft stems (calla, tulip etc.) supported by wire.

Florals: Tulipa-Hybriden, Dracaena fragrans., Viburnum opulus 'Sterile', Tillandsia xerographica, Echeveria agavoides, Equisetum palustre, Vanda Rothschildiana, Zantedeschia rehmannii, Anthurium-Andreanum-Hybriden, Rhipsalis capilliformis, Dichorisandra thyrsiflora, Hypericum calyc

**Description:**

Like a lush bouquet, raised on a container. With flowing, delicate structures. It reverses visual habits of floristry: The focal point and the weight are at the top, the bottom of the design becomes the base, the chassis.

**Application:**

Flower arrangement for a large, round table. A raised bouquet in a low dish and vase.

**Technique:**

Set in foam. Suppleness and flexibility of natural stems are used to create a lush optic at the top. The rosette made of horsetail is supported inside by wire. The upright bouquet can be worked with a round, gathered or any other base.

**Note:**

The meeting point and the focal area need not always be identical. However, in this case they are. The majority of the lines gather in the upper third; the bottom lines are less expressive and gather to an identical bundle.

Florals: Rosa-Hybriden, Lysimachia, Equisetum palustre, Hoya linearis, Jasminum officinale, Tillandsia usneoides

**Description:**

Several radial works which distinctly create a unity. Not only because of the same material and arrangement, but also because of their joint direction toward the center of growth which lies far below the base.

**Application:**

A parade of works on a wide or long surface is ideal for a table, stage apron, mantelpiece, gallery.

**Technique:**

Set in foam. Also tied into basic floral structure in strong group.

Florals: Salix caprea, Sandersonia aurantiaca, Tulipa-Hybriden, Hedera helix, Viburnum opulus 'Sterile', Echeveria agavoides

**Description:**

A powerful center. Compact. Dense. Threaded. Layered. Wrapped. Highly effective in small spaces due to circular ornament.

**Application:**

Bouquet for personal, emotional occasions. Also for dry and wedding floristry. Decoration on table, altar edge, etc. Tied, wired or simply set.

**Technique:**

Threaded on wire. Set in foam. In this case with wrapped ivy and a braid trailing over the edge of the table.

**Note:**

Threading floristry without water supply is only suitable for materials which dry without any major change in structure and color.

Florals: Rosa-Hybriden, Lunaria annua, Hedera helix, Ranunculus-Hybriden

**Description:**

Gathered. Layered. "Free" florals in between, which link and create focal points. Clever. Spontaneous. The craft is clearly visible.

**Application:**

Seasonal floristry, particularly for the autumnal season when there is a wealth of material to collect. Fresh and dry floristry. Bouquets. Arrangements.

**Technique:**

Various options: Speared on wood. Threaded on wire. Gathered with raffia, etc. Layered. Laid. Tied. Set in foam. And much more.

**Note:**

A fascinating structure which offers many creative details with limited means. Despite all the fascination this structure brings, the flowers should not be neglected. Nor should the careful and prudent handling of the floral be forgotten: Damaged parts of a plant depreciate the work.

Florals: Tulipa-Hybriden, Aeonium holochrysum, Galax aphylla, Lunaria annua, Xerophyllum asphodeloides

**Description:**

Bizarre. Sculptural. Original. Unconventional. Dominated by the structure. Exciting. Extreme yet leaving space for other things. Highly reduced presentation.

**Application:**

As decoration for thrilling dishes. For floral accents in a modern, reserved room design.

**Technique:**

Set in foam or on Kenzan. Tied with raffia. Tied in Rikka technique whereby the structure is placed on an underwater splint pin.

**Note:**
**The desire to draw attention to floral beauty calls for a reduction.**

Florals: Kalanchoe beharensis, Magnolia grandiflora, Kalanchoe tubiflora, Zygopetalon brachypetalum, Crassula rupestris

**Note:**
Besides the flower, other items can be the center of attraction: Like the near graphic design used here which supports its attractiveness.

**Description:**
Static. Even. Ornamental. Sequential. The plant subjects itself to the design. The flower adapts to the architecture, the order of the surrounding.

**Application:**
Wherever the plant recedes behind the expression of space and art: Art exhibitions. Altars.

**Technique:**
Included in wall or ceiling-suspended works. At or on stands. Or like here, mounted and leaning or suspended.

Florals: Phalaenopsis-Hybriden, Rhipsalis cassytha, Salix caprea

**Description:**

Heraldic. Graphic. Symbolic. Even. Drawn, as if with a meaning. Structures have space to unfold. Parallel lines.

**Application:**

Decoration in symmetrically structured, post-modern room designs: such as the typical architecture of the 80s with ornamentally-reduced structures (circle, rhombus, triangle, etc.)

**Technique:**

Set in foam, cover base with sand or moss.

**Note:**

This type of floristry is not very popular, yet in correlation with a respective ambiance it can prove surprising: hotels of exotic grace located by the ocean.

Florals: Heliconia, Lilium longiflorum, Aloe, Ranunculus-Hybriden, Kalanchoe tubiflora, Chamaerops humilis, Zantedeschia rehmannii, Galax aphylla

Florals: Heliconia, Rosa-Hybriden, Beaucarnea recurvata, Anthurium-Andreanum-Hybriden, Tillandsia usneoides, Dracaena indivisa 'Parey', Kalanchoe tubiflora, Nelumbo nucifera, Cornus alba sibirica, Hoya linearis

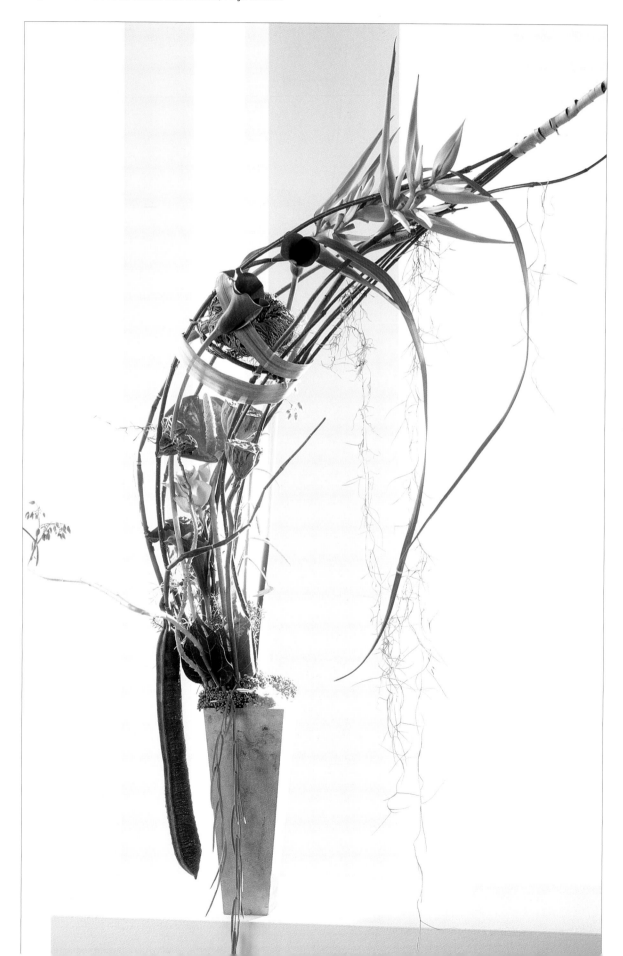

**Note:**
Diagonal structures cannot always be placed freely in a room. They often require an architectural element (here, the vertical division of the background) to set up a credible "visual point of reference".

**Description:**
Mounted. Anchored. Skillfully artificial. Dynamically breaking out of the central axis. Play with balance, density and dissolution. Each floral has its own zone of effect.

**Application:**
As a gift for unconventional recipients. Dry floristry. As floral object in a modern space.

**Technique:**
Tied with grapevine or raffia. Wired with jewelry wire in metallic colors. Set in foam. Placed in a vase like a bouquet.

Florals: Zantedeschia rehmannii, Protea optusifolia, Kalanchoe tubiflora, Cornus alba sibirica, Akacia, Nelumbo nucifera, Crassula rupestris, Leucadendron salignum

**Note:**
The play with balance
and visual habits and
clever and fresh
interpretations are also
a lot of fun for the floral
designer for a diagonal
line arrangement.

**Description:**

Drifting to the side. Floating. Exotic. Accentuated lines.
Growing from individual points. Single-weighted. Graphic.
Brought into structure in an unusual manner.

**Application:**

For a sideboard or a reception. On a mantelpiece. Wherever a
space is limited to the top but provides sufficient width.

**Technique:**

Set in foam. Tied freely in basic floral structure.

Note:
A widespread, more
contemporary and likeable
type of design – but
beware of its mannerism!

**Description:**
From different anchors in different volumes and dimensions, softly crossing, inter-flowing, then trailing florals.

**Application:**
On an elevated piece of furniture. On a mantelpiece, gallery, landing. For a sideboard. As altar decoration. Partition wall

**Technique:**
Set in foam. As short-cut bouquet tuff. Placed in mesh, set in Kenzan.

Florals: Zantedeschia rehmannii, Aristea cyanea, Muehlenbeckia complexa, Rosa-Hybriden, Lilium longiflorum, Salix matsudana 'Tortuosa', Galax aphylla, Hoya linearis

**Description:**
Fresh. Dynamic. Spontaneous "like magic". Unusual. Slanted. Modern.

**Application:**
Altar decoration. On a column or by a lectern. In correspondence with a slanted ceiling. Dried or fresh for wall decoration. Suspended in an elongated bowl.

**Technique:**
Set in foam. Tied freely with grapevine in basic structure then placed in elongated bowl with water.

Florals: Equisetum palustre, Ranunculus-Hybriden, Phormium tenax, Hedera helix 'Erecta', Curcuma amada, Zantedeschia rehmannii, Echinacea purpurea

**Description:**

Free. Natural cascade. Sprung out of a crevice; some climbers, dried florals from the previous year. The plants are not statically strung together but are carried along by the spontaneity of nature.

**Application:**

A natural accent in a modern, reduced room design. As discreet emphasis where other creations are to be in the forefront

**Technique:**

Set in foam, cover base with natural materials. Choose flat containers of discreet, plain shape and color.

**Note:**

**For the vegetative with downward proportions, the authentic recreation of the natural growth is what matters – nothing is imposed, pressed or pulled by force.**

Florals: Lysimachia, Tulipa-Hybriden, Jasminum officinale, Fallopia japonicum

**Description:**

Cool. Opposing. Interesting. Much structure, little color.
The free floral shape of the heliconia dominates,
the neat threaded material is only accompaniment.

**Application:**

Fresh and dried floristry with exotic flowers. In a vase but
also as a wall adornment.

**Technique:**

Rare combination of structure and craft; moreover pointed
downward. Layered. Threaded.

Florals: Heliconia, Rosa-Hybriden, Aristea cyanea, Crassula perforata, Rhipsalis cassutha, Cornus alba sibirica

Florals: Kalanchoe tubiflora, Aristea cyanea, Rhipsalis cassutha, Jasminum officinale, Phalaenopsis-Hybriden

**Description:**

Silhouettes thoughtfully winding downward. Interwoven foliage, climbers, flowers, unwinding in free fall.

**Application:**

On elevated positions: shelf, stand, column, mantelpiece, altar.

**Technique:**

Set in foam. Tied with grapevine or raffia into basic floral arrangement. Set in mesh made of natural materials. Often also tied to easily hold the winding.

**Note:**

When interweaving florals, the weaving is not only to be used as a base but also to lie above any possible flowers.

**Description:**

Like a memorial; sculptural presentation of life and death due to exciting blend of fresh and dried flowers. Dry floral support with the task of presenting the flowers living in water.

**Application:**

As a divider and a screen. On stands as ornamental indoor decoration. In a church as a wedding adornment. Excellent also as pure dry floristry. Freely suspended in a room; for walls multi-dimensional work is also feasible.

**Technique:**

Braided. Tied. Also glued. For fresh florals use water reservoirs.

Florals: Papaver nudicaule, Phyllostachys spec., Zantedeschia rehmannii, Muehlenbeckia complexa, Aristea cyanea

**Note:**
Especially for work of low height, the non-structural arrangement of lines provides an attractive tension due to the numerous angles and lines.

**Description:**

Order in chaos. Interesting and exciting: the freedom of lines in a clearly-defined system. What seems to criss-cross in the end only observes clear arrangement principles: The order is clarified, the design recognizable, preparations are decided on, the lines are freely arranged.

**Application:**

As a table decoration for conference tables and larger tables. On a divider. On a sideboard. Fireplace. Display window.

**Technique:**

Set in foam. Particularly attractive: Tied freely then placed in a flat container with water.

Florals: Liatris spicata, Rosa-Hybriden 'Black Beauty', Cestrum aurantiacum, Tulipa-Hybriden, Xanthorrhoea australis, Zygopetalon brachypetalum

**Description:**

Modern. Liberal, yet lush/ornamental. Despite the variety of material and strong groups, voluminous appearance. Formal-linear arrangement is definitely recognizable. The lines gather deep below the container which creates the impression of a major expansion at the top.

**Application:**

For indoor decoration. In a floor vase. Also for a more official occasion. For the presentation of goods in a shop. Long-lasting in warm premises.

**Technique:**

Set in foam, mesh, wire. As a bouquet with meeting point at the base.

Florals: Heliconia, Strelitzia, Anthurium-Andreanum-Hybriden, Muehlenbeckia complexa, Anigozanthos-Hybriden, Kalanchoe beharensis, Curcuma amada, Zantedeschia rehmannii, Strelitzia reginae, Ligularia japonica, Echinacea purpurea, Aeonium holochrysum, Cornus alba sibirica

**Note:**
The more reduced the arrangement, the more important the present elements: proportion, volume, length, depth, contrast – everything is of importance. Nothing can be overwritten or blurred, each floral "statement" must be adequate (see structural floristry).

**Description:**
Crossed lines trailing passively. Little structure in correlation of the to and fro. Dialogue of silhouette and personality, leaving the color in the background.

**Application:**
On an elevated point offering a front view. In a single or several flat dish(es) particularly in front of a design reduced in form and color, nearly bare backgrounds like concrete.

**Technique:**
Set in foam. Tied freely with grapevine or raffia.

Florals: Zantedeschia rehmannii, Zantedeschia aethiopica, Equisetum palustre, Cestrum aurantiacum, Lilium longiflorum, Rhipsalis cassytha, Aristea cyanea

**Description:**

Trilogy. Group of evenly related florals, each with their own meeting point. Width can be expanded to a row of several. Vertically stretched. Rhythmic. Focal point in the lower third.

**Application:**

For an altar, fireplace, mantelpiece. Stage apron. On a gallery. In an alcove.

**Technique:**

Set in foam. Tied, placed in a single vase.

**Note:**
Arrangements in several groups all have concurring segments, yet they also leave leeway. With highly ornamental arrangements this can also be used for precise, minute repetitions.

Florals: Agapanthus orientalis, Equisetum palustre, Aristea cyanea, Lilium longiflorum, Hyazinthus orientalis, Galax aphylla, Kalanchoe tubiflora, Muehlenbeckia complexa

Florals: Beaucarnea recurvata, Cornus alba sibirica, Kalanchoe tubiflora, Galax aphylla, Hyacinthus orientalis, Hedera helix 'Erecta', Agapanthus orientalis, Tulipa gesneriana

**Note:**

The difference between formal-linear and decorative arrangements sometimes is only based on the quantity of florals. The particular challenge of the arrangement shown is to ensure that the inclination to one side does not make the silhouette appear as if tilting.

**Description:**

Experimental. In contrast to visual conventions. Slanted to one side. Rich in shape yet reduced in volume. The bowed axis as a medium of surprise. Beside the flowers, the color green shows itself of equal significance. Even so, color is secondary, the structure dominates.

**Application:**

As an ornament in a modern, personal room.

**Technique:**

Tied as a bouquet. Set in foam or mesh. Tied freely.

Florals: Jasminum officinale, Salix caprea, Papaver nudicaule, Muehlenbeckia complexa, Leucothoe racemosa

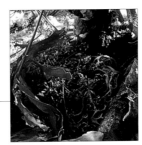

**Description:**

Like a piece of blooming nature. Small, medium-sized and large plants with little, more and many flowers. Here, too, the rule of the golden section structures the principles of nature.

**Application:**

As decoration in a modern room, very reduced, furnished with natural materials like wood, stone, raw iron, ceramics. Presented in a plain dish which replaces the natural location of the plants as discreetly as possible.

**Technique:**

Set in foam or Kenzan. Adapt base to natural ground of the tied-in flowers with stones, moss, sand, soil, fibers, a carpet of herbs.

Florals: Tulipa-Hybriden, Cornus alba sibirica, Xerophyllum asphodeloides, Viburnum tinus

**Note:**

Using structural designing is floristry which involves a lot of work and should therefore not be exaggerated and used only for the respective economic purpose – in dried floristry, for a wedding bouquet or for Christmas floristry.

**Description:**

Stylized. Like a sculpture. Broken through. Wrapped. Tied. Linked. The assembly dominates, few liberal florals accentuate. Fully natural, yet slightly stylized and artificial. Varying proportions to the side (asymmetry). Here, the structure of the floral dominates, but vice versa is also feasible.

**Application:**

To occupy a container. As a bouquet. As a small floral accessory in a modern interior. Occasionally also for wedding floristry.

**Technique:**

Winding floral fibers, bark, root, grapevine, grass. Also non-floral materials feasible: metal thread, wool, etc., in conjunction with a basic floral structure.

**Note:**

This type of work can have a very surprising effect which, however, is not based on the choice of florals but on the unconventional combination of the line arrangement and proportions.

**Description:**

Like an insect. Clearly separated forms become visible; bizarre, thin, trailing. Delicate and discreet in volume, density and color.

**Application:**

Discreet altar decoration. As indoor decoration, on sideboards or window sills. As fresh or dried design with preferably florals of highly contrasting effect.

**Technique:**

Set in foam. Tied freely with grapevine or raffia. Here: equisum stalks supported from within by wire, then bent. Place orchids which are difficult to set in foam in glass or natural tubes.

Florals: Curcuma, Phalaenopsis-Hybriden, Zantedeschia aethiopica, Equisetum palustre

Florals: Equisetum palustre, Senecio, Solanum, Sandersonia, Muehlenbeckia complexa

**Description:**

Slanted. Stacked. Like a parcel. Compact and dense. Filigree balance through motion with counter motion. Floral carpet elevated on natural water tubes.

**Application:**

As spectacular and effective table decoration consuming only little space, for relatively small surfaces. As buffet or sideboard decoration. Either fresh or dried arrangements.

**Technique:**

Set in foam. Short florals in natural stems or directly into foam. Tied to a parcel with raffia, grapevine or other aids.

**Note:**

This surprising method of using "water tubes" also facilitates watering the plants, since overflowing water is absorbed by the foam foundation and by the receptacle.

Florals: Ligularia japonica, Papaver nudicaule, Zantedeschia rehmannii, Aristea cyanea, Cymbidium-Hybriden, Euonymus europaea

**Description:**

Like a braid. A unity moving to one side, which nonetheless clearly shows individual details in shape. A work whose shape prescribed the will to a "low", nearly creeping motion.

**Application:**

A horizontal table decoration in modern but also rustic rooms: On lengthy items of furniture or also room elements like sideboards. Can be performed with many winding floral materials: long climbers, long, elastic foliage, grass, roots, fibers.

**Technique:**

Set in foam or mesh. Tied freely with grapevine or raffia. Free inter-winding on flat bowls, plates, containers. In combination with lying florals.

**Description:**

Romantic. Evokes images of the "past": Old gates, old fences with climbing plants which have dried out and returned. The notion of time is visibly incorporated: Old, confused, revived through fresh plants.

**Application:**

For atmospheric scenes, to reminisce. As motif decoration on a table, a sideboard, etc. To emphasize a deliberately nostalgic, weathered ambience.

**Technique:**

Grown. Set. Wound. Tied.

**Note:**

Nostalgia is an emotional term and as such is not actually part of the structure.

Florals: 'Rose von Jericho', Jasminium officinalis, Rosa-Hybriden, Fallopia japonicum, Muehlenbeckia complexa

**Description:**

Nature setting off for the year: The first bushes are blossoming (hammer shrub), tulips are emerging in search of light; grass, herbs and uncovered roots climb and wind around one another. This is an example of vegetative arrangements from one of those countries which is not closed off from warmer zones by the alpine mountains. This work beautifully illustrates how a feel for the different combinations of florals within a vegetative design can differ according to regional particulars. For example, in Australia, tulips flower under palm trees, next to splendid orchids, with high succulents lending a little shade.

**Technique:**

Set in foam. Setting base made of natural materials which concur with the depiction of the show flora.

**Note:**

There is more than just the central European to illustrate a vegetative design. Any "floral realm" has its own region as to which florals can grow together.

Florals: Cestrum aurantiacum, Cryptomeria japonica, Hedera helix 'Erecta', Tulipa-Hybriden, Xerophyllum asphodeloides

**Description:**

Tied like a trailing carrier. Designed, with a few flowers carrying the arrangement. The woven base puts this arrangement into an interesting static order.

**Application:**

On columns or high items of furniture. This floristry is also of interest due to its handling: If florals are placed in water reservoirs or mesh in the basic design, then they can be exchanged more frequently.

**Technique:**

Designed in tied basic arrangement. Place flowers in tubes or set in foam.

**Note:**

Mastering difficulties in mechanics when departing from the base comprising the axis and lines requires a certain learning process. The gradual understanding of engineering processes and the carrying ability of floral materials is also personally an interesting experience in addition to being beneficial to the craft as such.

Florals: Cornus alba sibirica, Galax aphylla, Rhipsalis cassytha, Zantedeschia rehmannii, Phalaenopsis-Hybriden, Hoya linearis

**Note:**

This arrangement should not necessarily be listed in a book on principals of floral design since it marks the transition to another important principal in floristry: The emotional illustration of the handling of a flower.

**Description:**

Close to nature. Spontaneous. Sweet. Romantic. Poetic. A small idyll of country-house Zeitgeist.

**Application:**

As a gift. As decoration for personal, warm, emotionally important occasions.

**Technique:**

Set in foam or in other organic arrangement aids like mesh made of twigs, balls made of climbers, bundles of little sprigs, etc. Tied to a bouquet.

**Note:**

Arrangement poetic

Florals: Hippeastrum vittatum, Tulipa-Hybriden, Lavendula spicata, Kalanchoe tubiflora, Jasminium nudiflorum, Muehlenbeckia complexa,

Xerophyllum asphodeloides, Papaver nudicaule

**Natural Study**

Generating natural studies teaches a lot about how to handle plants and parts of the plant. Moreover, this is an important step when learning floral arrangements.
Here is an attempt to categorize this process:

1.) Learning the structure and all its consequences.

2.) Studying of growth and copying it in natural studies.

3.) Intensive studying of silhouettes and lines, then making form sketches.

4.) Confronting the emotional statement of plants and parts of plants.

Florals: Viola wittrockiana, Helleborus niger, Hippophae rhamnoides, Pachysandra terminalis

# Imprint

Publisher: FloralDesign Edition
by kriener-potthoff communications, 48155 Münster/Germany

Förderungsgemeinschaft Blumen GmbH
as commissioned by Bundesverband, the national German professional association of florists,
45897 Gelsenkirchen/Germany

Design and Floristry: Gregor Lersch, 53474 Bad Neuenahr/Germany

Photography: Ralf C. Stradtmann, 22299 Hamburg/Germany

Layout: kriener-potthoff communications, 48155 Münster/Germany

Copyright © 1999 FloralDesign Edition by kriener-potthoff communications gmbh, 48155 Münster/Germany
2005, 3rd edition, printed in Germany

Distribution: FloralDesign Edition by kriener-potthoff communications gmbh,
Münsterstraße 111, D 48155 Münster, phone: +49(0)25 06/93 09-0, fax: +49(0)25 06/93 09-50,
e-mail: info@floraldesign-edition.com

ISBN 3-938521-10-4

## I say thank you

- to all colleagues, teachers and those in the floral profession who are deeply thoughtful – people who have previously worked on the substance of this book and those who have been teaching its contents day to day.

- to Ralf C. Stradtmann, my partner of many years, for his photographs.

- to Sabine Homering, graphic designer, who designed not only this book but also other publications of mine.

- ... and to my garden, who did its best so that we could work.

I dedicate this book to Alfred Voss who took on my work long before anybody else was willing to take a look at it, and who was always there for me; who let me grow, and pruned me, whenever necessary. Thank you.

Gregor H. Lersch